In *Hats, Clowns, and Miracles,* you will discover a woman who has indeed worn many hats in her lifetime. However, you will never think of a hat size as she tells her story. Rather, you will think of nothing but her heart size. Within Marcia's heart you will find the love of God that enables her to embrace family, friends, and even strangers, whatever the circumstances of life may bring. Blessings to all who read.

—John R. Parrott, Jr., associational missionary, Holston Valley Baptist Association, Rogersville, Tennessee

I know you will be blessed by this book. I know you will laugh and cry, but most of all you will be blessed.

—Nancy Lawson, Encourager Class ladies' Sunday school teacher, The Encourager radio program

HATS
CLOWNS &
MIRACLES

Natalie,

Still a sweet
sweet friend. So great
to see you again. May you
always have an incredible
& glorious joy in Jesus.

1 Peter 1:8

~ Marian ×
~ Clementine "
[signature]

HATS
CLOWNS &
MIRACLES

///

MARCIA "CLEMENTINE" MANIS

Tate Publishing *& Enterprises*

Published by Tate Publishing & Enterprises, LLC
127 E. Trade Center Terrace | Mustang, Oklahoma 73064 USA
1.888.361.9473 | www.tatepublishing.com

Tate Publishing is committed to excellence in the publishing industry. The company reflects the philosophy established by the founders, based on Psalm 68:11,
"The Lord gave the word and great was the company of those who published it."

Book design copyright © 2010 by Tate Publishing, LLC. All rights reserved.
Cover design by Kellie Southerland
Interior design by Stefanie Rooney

Published in the United States of America

ISBN: 978-1-61566-797-0
1. Biography & Autobiography, Women
2. Biography & Autobiography, Clowns
10.02.02

Dedicated to encouragers,
may we all be one.

Acknowledgments

Wow! My first book, and you helped make it possible. *Thank you* is a term that is often used flippantly, but I assure you that *thank you* is only the beginning of how I feel about each person who encouraged me to write my story and pursue publication. And now here we are!

To my Bible study group: You ladies are great! I love our fellowship and sharing time. Thanks for letting me share my stories and urging me to go for it!

To my friend Ann: Aren't you glad we are finally here? Maybe now your ears can get some rest. Thanks for lending them to me so many times.

To my Zula: What can I say? Thanks for sharing your days with a crazy clown and for sharing your gift of laughter with others.

To Tate Publishing: For your belief in me and that someone will read the words from my heart, I thank you.

To my loving family: You are the best! What else can be said? I could not have done this without you, and I would not have wanted to. I love you and thank you for believing in me.

To the family of Nancy Lawson: No one can ever take her place. She was my encourager and friend. I will always miss her, but I am so thankful that she is not lost to us because we know where to find her—with Jesus.

And of course, you! Yes, you! For taking the time to sit down, take some time from your busy day, and read a book. I hope you find encouragement and the love of Jesus in these pages.

TABLE OF CONTENTS

Foreword

When asked to write this foreword, I was honored. Having known Marcia for more years than I care to recount, I have a wealth of information to pen. However, let me just say that she is a joy to be around. Her little mind is always clicking; you can almost hear it—click, click, click. She should oil it and it wouldn't be so noisy. There is always a new friend to introduce, or new material, or a costume for an old friend. She can step in and out of character mode faster than I can think. She is not schizophrenic, though she portrays many personalities in her clown ministry. Regardless of which character you face when you see her, you can be assured of one thing: Each of these characters has a heart that is filled with the love of Jesus. That's what makes her so special. No matter what she is going through, it is evident that she is not alone. She makes it known in no uncertain terms that she trusts Jesus Christ as her Lord and Savior. He has gifted her to minister to others in a special way.

Thanks, Marcia, for entertainment, encouragement, and enlightenment. You and all the characters you portray are a blessing.

Love in Christ,
Doug Seymore, pastoral assistant and music director, East Rogersville Baptist Church

Introduction

How do you do? My name is Gertrude—no, Betsy—no, Mrs. Claus—no. Okay. Tonya Letha Lagonda, but you can call me Golly. How does one introduce oneself when one is not sure who one is? I do know one thing; I'm a sinner saved by grace.

Isn't it amazing to you that God knows all about us and knows exactly what is going to happen in our lives? Sometimes—most of the time—God's plans catch us off guard. We have our lives all planned and know exactly what we are going to do. Then, God jumps in and tells or shows us a different way—the way he wants us to go. Writing a book certainly caught me off guard.

A book! *Yes, I'm going to write a book.* The reactions of my family were mixed when I announced that I was planning to write a book. The first person I told was my daughter, Julie. She had come by with my little grandson Garrett to pick me up for lunch. Her reaction was, "Am I going to be in it?"

"Well, of course you are," I replied. I think she is still concerned that I will tell all our family secrets. I am only going to tell most of them.

My husband was the second person I told. His reaction was a giggle and, "Okay." Very complacent. Bless his heart. He never knows what I'm going to be up to next, but I know he will support me the best way he can.

My son was the third person I told. "Go for it, Mom, and don't procrastinate. Start writing." He is always my encourager, but I wish he would clean up his room and not procrastinate about that. Oh well.

Thus begins the journey of writing this book. I certainly never thought that I would ever be doing this. But then, I never thought I would do a lot of things in my life.

My book is about life—one woman's journey through it—plain and simple, with a lot of details: some fun, some sad, some a little crazy. All written with the intention of encouraging others to find true joy in life; the joy that only Jesus can give, no matter what the circumstance may be.

Easter Bonnets, Tiaras, and Cowboy Hats?

t all began, I would say, about fifty-five years ago. I certainly don't remember it, but my upcoming birth became a regular topic of conversation. I was born on Monday, May 5, 1952. Monday's child is fair of face (proven true—had lots of sunburns). My mother said I was due earlier, but *she* decided to wait until her doctor returned from an out-of-town trip for my delivery.

I know I was stared at a lot, and they made a lot of googly eyes at me and cooed and said, "Isn't she cute!" (I have pictures to prove it.) My mother said she wanted a bald-headed baby boy, but what they got was a red-headed baby girl. My parents were married around seven years before I was born and weren't used to keeping up with a little person. They thought they might leave me somewhere unknowingly. I don't think that ever happened, and if it did, they certainly never told me. I must have been something either very special or hard to duplicate because I was the only child they were blessed with during their marriage.

My toddler years were spent in Indiana. At the age of two my parents moved to Bristol, Virginia. Bristol is a split city—one part is in Virginia, the other in Tennessee. We also lived on the Tennessee side; but enough about geography.

I enjoyed my childhood. As a matter of fact, I don't think I ever really grew up. Being a child in the fifties and sixties was wonderful. We lived in typical suburban homes in typical suburban subdivisions. All of them were neatly planned and had neat names like East Road, Mt. Tucker, and Lamplighter Subdivision (with gas lights, of course). I'm sure many people my age can relate to all of the wonders of childhood during this wonderful era.

Our parents grew up during the Depression years and then war years. They wanted more for themselves and their families. They moved from the farms to the cities and found jobs in factories. My dad was one of those young men. He served in the navy on a supply ship in the South Pacific during World War II. I don't recall him ever speaking about the war, or even the navy, for that matter. He was a joyous, loving, and caring person, and I was his little girl.

I loved subdivision life. It was fun. Since I was an only child, a lot of my days were spent playing by myself. I never got *bored* like children do today. I had (and still have) a great imagination. I was an Indian princess in the wild west (my mother made me a papoose carrier to carry my baby in on my back); Rapunzel in the castle tower, who let down her hair for her prince to rescue her (the mimosa tree in the front yard and strips of material held with bobby pins attached to my hair); a teacher with dolls for students. I loved to play with my dolls, have tea parties (I still do), read books, and ride my bicycle.

Of course, like all children, I had mishaps. Like the time my cousin Charlene decided it would be a grand idea if we both got inside my pedal car and rode down the hill in the backyard. This would have been a wonderful idea, except for a few things. *One:* it was a very steep hill. *Two:* my swing set was at the bottom of the hill. *Three:* no brakes on a pedal car.

Charlene decided to give me a little push and then jump in—she never made it. As I raced down the hill, I tried to stop, but I was going so fast that I couldn't even manage to get my feet on the pedals, and steering the thing was impossible. I remember seeing bushes and trees (and my short life pass before me) and then *thump, bounce, bang.* I had hit the corner of the swing set, bounced out, and hit my head.

Charlene, in the meantime, had run to the house and announced she had killed me and I was at the bottom of the hill. I don't remember much after that, except there was an ice pack on my eye and I had the biggest, blackest shiner you have ever seen.

One good thing about subdivisions is other kids. There were always kids around. Most of them were either older or younger than I was, so I adapted. The family next door had four children. They had a set of twins (boy and girl) who were about three, a daughter my age, seven or eight, and an older daughter who was a preteen. The girl who was close to my age was a tomboy. She loved climbing trees and playing cowboys and Indians. I, of course, was the Indian princess. The twins were a constant delight. They were, of course, mischievous and lots of fun.

They thought my parents could fix anything. My mother was the doctor. If they had a boo-boo, they ran to our house to get a Band-Aid and a cookie or something to forget the pain. My dad was the dentist, and when they had a loose tooth, he pulled it. One night the little boy announced to his family that he was running away. He packed his pj's in a paper bag and promptly ran away to our house. After a long conversation with my dad, he decided it might be a good idea to go back home before it got dark.

The family who lived across the street was very interesting as well. Their house was small, yet it held ten children (all boys) ranging in age from four to around fourteen, two German shepherds, a cat, and a crow with a broken leg, and most of the time they all played amongst themselves. I played with the youngest children who were closer to my age. They usually came to my yard and played because I was afraid of the dogs.

I guess my earliest encounter with death was when their youngest boy found a nickel on the playground at school and ran across the highway to the Minute Market to buy something. He was hit by a car and died. The rest of the time that they lived there, even the crow seemed sad.

Some of the other neat things about growing up in the fifties were the music (rock and roll), the clothes (crinolines, black patent shoes, ruffled socks), hairstyles (ponytails, bangs, and bobs) party lines on the phone, cars and houses with open-window air conditioning, and food (Krispy Kreme donuts, hot dogs at the Dog & Suds). It was certainly a unique time in our culture.

I always wore dresses to school, and I liked it. Pants at that time weren't allowed. I especially loved to dress up on Sunday. I loved wearing frilly dresses, my crinoline under my dress, my ruffled socks, gloves, and my black patent shoes. I had problems with my feet as a child and wore ugly brown, tied-up shoes to school, so I felt especially pretty on Sunday with my cool shoes. My mother always fixed my hair on Saturday night—pin curls so tight they made my eyes stretch. I wore my hair net to keep it all in place: no curling irons or blow dryers. I looked like Shirley Temple most of the time.

And then on Easter Sunday, the coolest thing of all—a corsage and a hat! I guess I fell in love with hats when I was just a tot; they were so fashionable, after all. They were the crowning glory on a woman's head. You looked so coordinated from head to toe. Of course, your handbag had to match your hat and your shoes. I mean, it was a well-orchestrated event!

Bonnets, headbands, and all kinds of hat-wear were okay with me. I wore a bonnet when I was a baby, and I wore a bonnet when I was in a play at school. One of the songs was "Billy Boy." "Oh where have you been, Billy Boy, Billy Boy? Oh where have you been, darling Billy?" I was one of the girls in the chorus singing the song, and we all wore long dresses and bonnets. It was the neatest thing ever!

In my teenage years, I still wore hats; pillbox, of course. They were the latest thing, and the president's wife started the trend, so you knew it had to be cool! Why, my Barbie dolls even had pillbox hats made by my cousin from little nut-cups covered in fabric.

And what about vacations! We would usually leave for vacations in the middle of the night; mainly because it was cooler to drive at night (remember, no air conditioning). I got so excited before we left that I couldn't sleep. I always looked forward to leaving because it meant that I got to sit in the front seat with my dad. Mom liked lying down in the backseat while we were traveling. I guess she was exhausted from packing and getting ready to leave. My dad and I talked, and he loved to sing. My favorite times were in the car with him singing songs like "Buffalo gal, won't you come out tonight," and "Pickin' up paw-paws, putting 'em your Pocket," and "Rock of Ages." We would stop at a roadside diner so he could get a cup of coffee, and I, of course, had a grilled Krispy Kreme donut. My dad loved to travel. We went to the beach, the mountains, or to visit relatives. It was always fun, and those were times I'll never forget.

Yes, I enjoyed being a child and everything that went with it; riding bikes, going to school, and playing with friends, but one of the most wonderful things was going to church. My parents always took me to church—they didn't *send* me. They went with me. I guess my earliest recollection of church was children's church. I loved the Bible stories they told on a felt board, and I came home and cut out paper dolls and construction paper, draped a blanket over pillows on the couch, and placed my dolls in a row on the floor. I imagined that I was the teacher and tried to tell the stories to my dolls like they had been told to me.

I loved Vacation Bible School, especially the stories about missionaries, and the crafts we made were always so much fun. And *music!* I loved to sing. I still love to sing! Music can touch your soul like nothing else. When I need a spiritual lift, I listen to music. I loved the songs I sang as a child, "Jesus Loves Me" and "Let the Sun Shine In." I loved the hymns we sang, "Amazing Grace," "Rock of Ages" (my dad's favorite), "Tell Me the Story of Jesus," "Victory in Jesus," "Open My Eyes," and "Heavenly Sunshine."

I loved church (still do) and everything about Sundays. I loved spending time with my parents, having a big Sunday dinner, and maybe having a special friend over to play with on Sunday afternoons. I grew up in a grand time. Life could not have been more perfect.

Little did I know that my life would soon change and never again be the same.

//

When I was a child, I spoke as a child, I understood as a child, I thought as a child; but when I became a man, I put away childish things.

1 Corinthians 13:11 (NKJV)

Salvation's Miracle

The summer before I was to enter seventh grade, we moved to Oak Ridge, Tennessee. My father had already been working for several months at the Oak Ridge National Laboratory.

I really liked Oak Ridge. We lived in an apartment complex. There were three other families in our complex. A young couple in their early thirties lived above us with their little boy. This was my first time baby-sitting, and I thoroughly enjoyed it. He was around two years old, had been born with some problems with his legs, and had a late start learning to walk. He was a delight, and my whole summer was filled with visits to his apartment, amidst riding my bike and just generally having fun.

By the end of the summer, my parents had decided to move to Indiana. My dad was not comfortable with the radiation he was being exposed to at Oak Ridge. Thus began my seventh-grade year at Noblesville Junior High School. I made lots of new friends and adapted well to my surroundings. Noblesville was made up of many people who had moved from the south to find jobs in the north. Firestone had a plant in Noblesville, and twenty miles in either direction were General Motors and Delco-Remy. My dad worked for General Motors for a while and then eventually for Delco-Remy.

My life was pretty normal, if a preteen and teenager can have a normal life. I loved Noblesville. We were five minutes from the pool. The land was flat, so it was great for riding my bike and learning how to drive. Noblesville and the surrounding area at that time were made up of farmland, mostly dairy. I started dating one of the farm boys who went to my school, and our families became good friends. I learned how to square dance, and almost every Friday and Saturday night we would go to a dance. My parents took lessons, and it became a family affair. We built a new house, and everything seemed perfect.

In the middle of my sophomore year of high school, my parents decided to move to Arizona. My mother had some health issues, and the doctors had suggested she move to a warmer, drier climate. So off we went again! Although I had moved many times and had adapted fairly well, this time I wasn't as thrilled. I had some really close friends and loved the school I attended. I was tired of moving. Nevertheless, we moved to Glendale, Arizona (just outside Phoenix), and began a new life again.

Dad had taken the job over the phone, and what should have been a foreman's job that he was promised turned out to be a seven-day-a-week job. My mother had never learned to drive, so I became the chauffeur to the store, the mall, and anywhere else we needed to be.

The school was huge. There were as many kids in my class as there had been in my whole school in Indiana! It was hard to get to know very many kids, but I was beginning to adapt when— you guessed it—we moved again, back to Indiana. Dad was tired of working seven days a week, and we couldn't tell that the climate had made a great deal of difference in Mom's health. The weather was great in Phoenix, and I loved going back to Indiana with a great tan.

On our return to Indiana, we rented a house and then moved into a duplex and planned to build a house in the spring. Since we had come back to Indiana, my dad seemed tired all the time and began to lose some weight. In November of 1968, he finally relented and went to the doctor for a checkup. By Thanksgiving, we had the diagnosis: leukemia. We were told that he had no more than six months to live.

At that time, there was no cure for the type of leukemia he had, and blood transfusions became a way of life. I would take him to the hospital on Saturday for a cross-match of his blood and then back on Sunday for a transfusion.

Life had turned upside down, and I couldn't understand why this loving, caring man had to suffer. What kind of God lets that happen?

Please don't think I didn't love my mother. I did, and had great respect for her, but I was Daddy's girl. My mother was sick a lot, and we were just never as close as my dad and I. Mother didn't like to travel a lot, so when we made trips back to Tennessee to visit, it was usually just my dad and me. I loved spending time with him whenever I could. Every Saturday we would go to town and get the groceries, pay bills, and just hang out. I never tired of being with him. I can still see him standing next to me in church singing his favorite hymn, at the top of his voice.

He taught me how to love and care for others by his example. Daddy belonged to the Masons, and one year at Christmas, they were taking items to needy families. This particular year, he asked me to go along. The family lived in a barn with a packed-down dirt floor, yet the children were clean, and the family was appreciative of the food and items for the children.

I remember him saying to me, "Don't ever make fun of anyone that has less than you. God has blessed you, but these people are not any different in God's eyes." I respected and admired him for not only being my dad but for the unselfish care and love he showed others.

On March 1, 1969, at forty-six years of age, my father went home to be with the Lord. My world was shattered. I walked around for days, weeks at school, not knowing what to do or where to go. I had wanted to go to college and become a teacher. All that changed when he died.

My mother had not worked in years and then only part time. She had been a homemaker, wife, and mother. Daddy had paid all the bills and taken care of all the family matters. I immediately felt the responsibility to take over and try to find a part-time job to help with bills. I abandoned my plans to be a teacher and took all the business subjects I could get my hands on. I was angry and bitter that my world had changed and that the person I loved the most was gone. My dad had never been sick, and now in three short months, his life was over, and I felt that my life was over as well.

Dad had requested to be buried in Tennessee next to his brother, and my mother had decided that we would move there after I graduated from high school. She felt it was what Dad wanted, for us to be close to family. I did not want to leave. All my friends were in Noblesville. My last happy times with my dad were there. Graduation was a sad time, and I felt as if I were moving to a foreign country. We did. We moved the next day to Surgoinsville, Tennessee. Needless to say, Surgoinsville is not a large town; only one stoplight.

My cousin had found us a house to live in, and I immediately started looking for jobs.

Now, let me tell you about this house. It definitely had been neglected and was in need of repair. *One:* the shower looked as though it had not been cleaned in years, and the toilet was ready to fall through the floor. *Two:* no stove. My mother used the electric coffee pot to boil corn on the cob and fixed sandwiches for supper. *Three:* my room was on one side of the living room, and Mother's room was across the living room and across the entryway, on the other side of the house. *Four:* Rats. *Five:* fleas. Need I say more! Of course, we were not there a great deal. I was looking for a job, and we stayed at my cousin's house and slept on the floor after about two weeks of living at the flea house.

Our next home was at the historic Hale Springs Inn over the Sweet Shoppe. We were having a home built in Surgoinsville and were staying at the inn until it was finished.

I eventually got a job thirty miles away in Kingsport.

Every other day I begged Mother to move back to Indiana, or at least let me go. I hated Tennessee. I hated the way we lived. I wanted to go to college. I missed my friends. I missed my dad, and I was lonely. We were invited to go to a local church and attended there for several months. It was small, and there were very few young people.

In the meantime, I began dating a young man whose mother was a childhood friend of my mother. His sister had been saved at East Rogersville Baptist Church, and we were invited to come to the baptismal service. It was wonderful. The choir was filled with thirty, maybe forty young people who sang like nothing I had ever heard! I was hooked. I had to go back.

There was something unusual about this choir. They seemed to have a joy and a peace that I didn't have. Although I had grown up in church all my life and felt that I was saved (had asked Jesus to come into my heart), I knew that something was not quite right.

Our choir director was phenomenal. He not only led our choir but was a preacher as well. I had never been around anyone who was so thrilled about Jesus and wanted others to know him. Most of the churches I had grown up in were more formal. They were more structured; everything was on a schedule, and it was followed to the letter. I never saw a great deal of emotion in the churches I had attended. However, in this choir and in this church, people shared their testimonies and showed overflowing joy and happiness. I knew I didn't have what they had. I tried to remember a time when I had asked God to come into my life, and I couldn't. Yet everyone thought I was saved, I guess because I believed it as well.

When I was about eight, my best friend was saved, and of course, if my best friend was saved, I surely had to be saved too. I remember talking to my parents, and I am sure they explained it to me, and I probably had the head knowledge but not the heart knowledge. I had made the decision on a Sunday night to go forward in the church. My mom and dad went with me. I don't remember praying, although we might have. The preacher took my hand, and then I cried. My parents told me not to cry, yet they were crying. It didn't make sense to me, but I accepted the fact that I was saved. For years, I thought I was saved. Now I wasn't so sure.

I became involved in this wonderful church. I had always loved music, and the youth choir was great. I even sang a solo. I worked in children's church as the music leader and became involved with the bus ministry. I was going to *work* my way into heaven. The more I became involved and the harder I worked, the more God's Spirit was drawing me to him. But the devil was working hard as well, telling me I was all right.

A battle raged inside of me, and there were many, many restless nights. John Parrott, Jr., our choir director, was very perceptive. He noticed that I was troubled and asked me on different occasions what was wrong. I, of course, didn't want anyone to know that I might not be saved, so I said, "Nothing." Finally, he asked me if I was questioning my salvation, and I told him no. I couldn't question what I didn't have. John asked if he could have prayer with me, but I was so tormented by the devil and not sure what to do that I wouldn't even bow my head.

This went on for several months. One Sunday night, John asked me to sing a solo. I didn't want to do it, but I knew if I didn't, people would wonder why. I could hear John behind me, praying for me! How dare he! Why couldn't he just leave me alone?

In the fall of 1971, our church planned to have a revival. Bob Steele, a Virginia state trooper, was the evangelist. Wow! That's the best word to describe him. He had a presence and such a power in his voice that you knew God was with him. What do you think he preached on all week? Unsaved church members, of course! This was still a time when churches had a revival that lasted all week and maybe two or three weeks. I hoped and prayed this one wouldn't last long and I could get back to pretending to be a Christian. All week long, I sat toward the middle or back of the church and gripped the pew in front of me during the invitation. I refused to sing in the choir. Only a few people who were close to me knew that I was struggling with a decision. I had told them if they even mentioned to me about going to the altar and praying about salvation that I would not go.

One night during the revival, a special group was invited to sing. They sang "Getting Ready Today, Moving Out Tomorrow," and it spoke to my heart. A friend who knew I doubted my salvation said to me, "Don't you know you can't get ready tomorrow. Tomorrow is too late! You have to get ready today."

I knew the words were true. I knew I was lost, with no hope of a tomorrow, not even the promise of today. The devil was losing his grip. The last night of the revival, I sat toward the front of the church yet still gripped the pew. I knew this was my last chance to make peace with God. One of the young men in our church who knew me started to come out of the choir. I just knew he was coming to talk to me, and I could no longer stand under the pressure. Before he even reached where I was standing, I was on the altar, but there was still no peace. The evangelist prayed with me, talked with me, and my words to him were, "I can't."

Finally, John spoke with me and said these words. "You're right. You can't, but God can."

How easy it was! All I had to do was ask God to come into my heart and let *him* take over my life! Why hadn't I been able to do that before? Why had I made it so hard? There was instant peace and joy. No tears this time, just a peace that would last until eternity. I could move out any time and be ready to meet Jesus! I could hardly believe this miracle had happened to me.

Hallelujah! What a Savior!

For God so loved the world that he gave his only begotten Son, that whoever believes in Him should not perish but have everlasting life.

John 3:16 (NKJV)

Overflowing Joy

People we meet every day have an influence on our lives, as we have on theirs. We never know who we're going to affect by our actions, our speech, our walk, and our talk. Whether we realize it or not, each time we speak or meet someone, they form an opinion about us. Will that opinion be one in which they see Christ?

This chapter is about some of the people who have influenced my life in one way or another. I'm sure some of them never knew they were even making that impact, but I'm so thankful for each of them.

It's hard to say who had the most influence on my life. I think God placed all the people in my life he knew I would need to make me a better Christian.

Of course, I've already talked about my dad and how much I love him. Just as our heavenly Father is always with us, my dad was a constant in my life. He was next to youngest in his family and was raised on a farm in Sneedville, Tennessee. He came from a close family. Even though we moved a lot, he always made sure that I knew his family, and we visited them often. When I think of Daddy, I always see a smile on his face. Seldom did I see him without that smile.

He must have been mischievous when he was a child because it carried over into his adult life. He loved having fun and playing practical jokes on people. Daddy once told my cousin he wouldn't catch a fish unless he spit on his worm. Darryl promptly took his fishing pole out of the water and spit on his worm. Another cousin told of how my dad would watch his older brother Kyle preach and then go home, get the Sears catalog, go to the woods, find a stump, and pretend to preach just like him.

I seldom saw Daddy cry. He always tried to be strong for everyone, but there was one time in particular that I know his heart was broken. My cousin Mavis visited us often, and once stayed with us when we had a car accident. When Mavis was twenty-seven years old, she was diagnosed with cancer. My dad and I made a trip to Tennessee to see her during Christmas break. She was so frail and weak. She also had two small children she was trying to care for. By the time we were able to go visit, she could no longer care for the children. She spent most of her days in bed. In only a few short months, she was gone. Dad was heartbroken, and I remember how he grieved over the loss of her young life.

I am so glad for the short time I had with my father. He showed me that life is joyous and wonderful and that we should never take it for granted.

There have been some special women in my life as well. One was my grandmother Price. Let me see if I can describe her. She was a stocky woman with snow-white hair who wore a bonnet and smoked Prince Albert tobacco in her pipe. Yes, she smoked a pipe! I have only seen a few pictures of her as a young woman, and she was striking. I imagine she had long flowing hair because her hair was done in the Gibson girl style. She was taller than my grandfather. He was probably around five feet five inches and wore a handlebar mustache. They made a handsome couple. Together they raised ten children.

By the time I came along, my grandfather had died, and all their children were grown. She lived on a little ridge across the creek from her son. Going to her house was always fun. She would dote on me and let me eat cookies, and talking to her was like talking to someone who understood me.

My favorite times were when my cousin Doris came over to my grandmother's house. We would make up little plays or pretend we were giving a concert. The bedroom was our rehearsal area, and the curtain door was our stage. Grandmother would wait patiently for us to appear, and whatever we did, she would applaud and make us feel like we had just stepped out on Broadway. She loved it best when we sang hymns, and she often sang with us. She gave me unconditional hugs, kisses, and encouragement.

Another lady in my family who always made me feel welcome was my dad's sister, Della Fain. Oh how I loved to go see her! She lived on a farm as well and would feed all the farm hands. I have never seen so much food in my life. I think that is where I fell in love with food. She could cook anything and it would be delicious, but the thing I loved the most was her corn on the cob. I don't know what she did to it, but it would melt in your mouth!

Her house was always full with farm hands or children or just someone visiting. I know they never left hungry. Cooking was her gift, and she shared it with anyone who came to her door. I often went to church with Aunt Della when we came to visit and saw in her face and spirit the love she had for others. Her joy for God was ever present, and I loved her dearly.

Teachers in my life made a great difference. I guess my favorite was my fourth-grade teacher, Mrs. Holt. We also went to the same church. She was a tall, gray-haired lady who always dressed with style and smelled wonderful.

I loved her class. She made each one of us feel special. I loved to read, and it seems that in fourth grade, there was a lot of reading to be done. A little boy in our class was struggling with his reading and spelling words. Mrs. Holt asked if anyone in the class would give up their recess time to stay in and help him. I volunteered. I don't know why. Maybe because Mrs. Holt enjoyed helping us so much that I wanted to see what it would be like to help someone else. Several weeks went by, and it was time for the big spelling test. I knew I would pass, but I was thrilled when the little boy made a good grade as well. I knew it was because I had helped. He was so proud of his accomplishment. Later I learned that this little boy was from the same family my dad and I had visited who lived in the barn.

There was a presence about Mrs. Holt that everyone loved. She not only was a great teacher but wife and mother as well. She had two sons and a beautiful daughter, Linda. One Sunday at church, I saw Mrs. Holt and her husband leave church early. At the end of the service, we were told her daughter had been involved in a fatal car accident. She had been on her way to pick up her fiancé at the airport when a milk truck crossed the centerline and hit her car head on. She was a beautiful girl, and I remember going to the funeral home. She was dressed in her prom dress, and her head lay on a beautiful lace pillow. Even though I'm sure Mrs. Holt was devastated, she seemed very strong. She was a Christian, and her faith sustained her.

Years later when I moved back to Tennessee, I had lost a child. Mrs. Holt called me with words of encouragement and sent flowers to ease my pain. I know she offered up prayers for me and kept me in her thoughts.

Mrs. McFarland was my junior high and high school music teacher. She was average height and had short, dark, straight hair and a fire and passion in her eyes that you noticed the first time you met her. I loved her class. She pushed us to the limit, made us sit up straight and hold our hands and arms a certain way. She was great. Most of all, she made us love music because she loved music. It was her passion. We learned all kinds of music—folk music, classical music. Her favorite music was church music. They weren't just hymns to her; they were sounds from heaven. Although hymns probably aren't sung as much at schools now, in my day, it was encouraged. We presented concerts to the school and often went to churches in the area as well.

Mrs. McFarland always took the time to listen if you had a problem and made you feel as though you were the only student she had. Her Christianity showed in the way she cared for others and her passion for singing praises to him.

Mr. Nugent was not one of my teachers. I didn't have any of his classes. I belonged to FTA (Future Teachers of America), and one of our duties was to help the teachers in whatever capacity they needed. I was assigned to Mr. Nugent. I stayed after school a couple of times a week and helped him grade papers and just do general work for him in his classroom. He was always kind. He was very tall (at least six feet two inches), had white, crew-cut hair, and always wore a suit. He never talked a lot, but he always smiled. He was a gentle giant. He knew that my dad was very sick and often asked how he was doing. Just before Christmas break, Mr. Nugent handed me an envelope with some money in it and told me to use it to buy something for my mom and dad for Christmas. I guess he knew that times were hard for us, and I suppose I had mentioned getting them something for Christmas. I will never forget his kind gesture and what it meant to me to be able to get something for my parents on what would be our last Christmas as a family.

I have visited Indiana several times and on

several occasions have been able to speak with Mr. Nugent and let him know how much I appreciated the kindness he showed toward my family and me. Sometimes we may never know the impact little things we do for people can mean to their lives. Mr. Nugent's words and very presence showed Jesus in his life.

John Parrott, Jr., was and is someone who truly has shown me what a Christian should be. John was a one of a kind youth leader and song director. He was so in love with Jesus that it naturally showed in his words and actions. We had choir practice on Monday nights, and I could hardly wait. It was singing practice, prayer, and praising. When we sang at our church, or at any church, John encouraged us not only to sing but to give our personal testimony as to how we were saved or whatever the Lord laid on our hearts.

His enthusiasm for telling others about Jesus caught on like wildfire, and you couldn't help but want to be a part of it. Not only did he lead our choir, he taught the college Sunday school class, taught our training union class, and led visitation for the youth. He knew the Bible and was not afraid to stand up for his faith, no matter where he was. He told us to be bold for Jesus. We saw many souls saved and lives changed through the youth ministry of our church. I was one of those lives that was changed because someone like John stood for Jesus and followed where the Lord was leading him.

Ed Shanks was our children's church pastor, and his wife, Ruth, was always there to support and encourage him. They did not have children of their own, but on Sunday morning, every child in the church was their child. Our church started a bus ministry, and before long, we had an abundance of children. We had over one hundred children in the eight-to-eleven age group alone. At nineteen, I became involved with the bus ministry and with children's church.

I believe God only picks very special people to work with children. Ed always took time for the children, answered their questions, and put loving arms around them. He taught them about Jesus and told about salvation on a child's level so they could understand. He was wonderful, and the children loved and respected him. He organized special trips for the children, and there were always incentives to learn Bible verses. Ed and

Ruth became my surrogate parents. They always made me feel like their special teenager. They were there to encourage me through the trials of dating and in my Christian walk with the Lord. I learned a great deal from them and feel blessed to have been able to work with them to further God's kingdom. They will have a special mansion filled with children because of their love and faithfulness to God.

Preacher Bill Brown was one of the best encouragers I have ever known. My mother passed away just before he became the pastor of our church. I needed encouragement, and he offered his help on more than one occasion. Since I was the junior choir leader and the leader of our clown ministry, I was always coming up with things to do.

Preacher Bill never said no to anything I asked him to do in a church service. One particular time was when the children were going to do a song that had a western melody. I asked him to just go with whatever I was going to be doing that Sunday morning with the children and assured him he wouldn't be too embarrassed. Now you need to get the picture for this. Preacher Brown was average height, but his head was a little larger than most people, and he had a short neck. His head was perfect for a child's cowboy hat, and of course, he had to swing a rope like a real cowboy. His part was the *yahoo* at the end of each verse. He was great! He yahooed loud and swung the rope like a pro. The children and adults loved it.

On another occasion, I had come up with a new character that I wanted to try in church. When I told him that this character came to me during the night, his reply was, "You're not having visions, you're having nightmares." Yet one Sunday morning, he allowed me to bring that character to life and hopefully make people think about their lives as Christians.

Preacher Bill not only preached the Word but presented the gospel with different illustrations and props during his sermon. He sometimes took a new and different path to tell us an old and wonderful story about Jesus. I will never forget his encouragement, his love for life, and his joy in sharing the Word of God with others.

I guess the running theme for this chapter has been *joy:* Jesus first, Others second, Yourself last. All of the people in this chapter had an overflowing, everlasting joy that spilled over into the lives of others. That *joy* is Jesus! I am so blessed God chose to put them in my path and draw me closer to him. Jesus is joy unspeakable and full of glory!

//

Though you have not seen him, you love him; and even though you do not see him now, you believe in him and are filled with an inexpressible and glorious joy.

1 Peter 1:8 (NIV)

Wedding Veil

"All you need is love," so says the popular song. That is so true when you first fall in love, then after about a year you find out you have to eat and pay bills! Jim Manis is the love of my life. Let me tell you our love story.

As a teenager, I felt very homely. I wore glasses, was skinny (hard to believe, I know), and had short hair. I did not date much, only one or two boys in high school. I was nineteen when we moved to Tennessee, and by the time Jim and I met, I had blossomed a little and had long hair but was still skinny. We met at church. He had recently come back from Vietnam and renewed his relationship with the Lord. He attended East Rogersville Church and sang in the youth choir. I really wasn't too interested in him, but evidently, he had his eye on me.

One night after church, my girl friend and I rode around town and circled the local hangout, the Po Boy. Jim and his friend Al Karst were sitting in their car and motioned for us to come alongside and wanted us to go for a ride. Now mind you, we didn't know these guys very well. We had barely spoken. Jim told Al he wanted the girl with the blondish hair to sit with him.

We discussed important and intellectual things, like pizza, movies, and bowling. We drove out to Pressman's Home. Some local girls had told me that Pressman's Home was where boys took girls to make out and stuff. I thought, *Great, this guy is going to make some moves on me that I don't want, and I'll be in the middle of nowhere and no way to get out of it! Help!*

I was pleasantly surprised. Jim Manis didn't even try to kiss me. I was so impressed. What a gentleman!

We dated on and off for about a year; sometimes more off than on. You see, Jim wasn't quite sure he wanted to settle down yet. I, however, knew he was the one from the first time he kissed me on a little country road. He had the warmest smile and the most beautiful, soulful, brown eyes I had ever seen. And he was handsome and smart. He could have any girl he wanted.

During the latter part of our courtship, I caught him with another girl when we were supposed to have a date later that night. I told him we were through. I cried for days and just knew I would end up a spinster old maid.

Two weeks passed. Jim knew I didn't want anything to do with him. It was over, and I knew I would have to get on with my life. I was tired of the yo-yo relationship we were having. He would call and I would hang up. Finally, he had Al call and sweet talk me into talking to him. I didn't have a lot to say, but he continued calling.

Then one night, he called and said he was going to see me the next day or else. During this time, my mother was not very fond of him. Her exact words were, "If he comes up here, I'm calling the law." I convinced him not to come to the house and said I would meet him after he got off work that night. Now I had to tell my mother. I waited until we were in a restaurant so she couldn't yell at me. She didn't say anything.

I met Jim that night, and we rode around and talked and talked. He asked for forgiveness, and at first I was reluctant to forgive him. Then he took me in his arms, looked at me with those beautiful eyes, and kissed me. I was in heaven! You know, girls! You've been there if you've ever been in love.

Most of this talking was done in the driveway at his house, and when I started my car to go home—you guessed it: I had a broken water hose. Jim had to take me home, which meant since this was Saturday night, he would have to pick my mother and me up for church on Sunday morning. I couldn't sleep. I just knew she would rake him over the coals for the way he had treated me.

But on Sunday morning, it was as if honey had melted in her mouth. "How are you, Jim?"

"Fine, and you?" I could have killed them both. On Monday Jim had my car fixed, and I had to take him back home to get his own car. As we drove by the Hawkins County Farmers Co-op, he said, "Let's get married."

I said, "Okay, when?"

"Friday night okay?"

"Okay." Thus the proposal. Very romantic.

Two weeks later on Friday, July 7, 1972, in

the living room of my mother's home, I became Mrs. Jim Manis. I have been married thirty-five years and don't regret a day I have spent with this incredible, loving, sensitive man. Granted, there have been times I wanted to kill him, but I never have regretted the love and times we have shared.

A week after we were married, though, I wasn't as confident as I am now. *What have I done? I don't know this person, and he really doesn't know me.* I would never have told my mother I made a mistake. I didn't want to hear, "I told you so."

Her advice about marriage was, "Remember, you're not marrying a relative, it's a complete stranger." It's true. You really don't know that person until you live with them, but what a joy for that stranger to become your best friend. And as for poor Jim, he is the one who got the stranger. For one thing, he didn't know I couldn't cook. I really had never had to do much cooking at home, but I thought as a good wife, it was my duty to give it a try. Jim probably wished I had tried on someone else. The first breakfast I fixed for him was just a regular breakfast: burned eggs, burned bacon, burned toast. I couldn't mess up the juice.

I cried and begged him not to eat it. He said,

"It's all right, it's good, it's the way I like it." Later, I overheard him tell my brother-in-law, "I had to eat it. I felt so sorry for her." Now, that's love.

Then there was the time that the pastor and his wife came by to visit the newlywed couple. We had been otherwise engaged before Jim answered the door. I begged him not to answer, but it was too late. They had seen our car and knew we were home. It was obvious to them what had transpired, and Jim, wonderful husband that he is, suggested he needed to go outside and get some firewood for the fireplace. The pastor said no, but Jim insisted. We didn't need a fire, and besides, it was pouring down rain—the wood was wet! The pastor and his wife just laughed, and I sat there so embarrassed I just wanted to hide under a rock. Jim, on the other hand, was just standing in the rain. He eventually came back in, and they soon left. It's funny now, but at the time we were both mortified.

Jim also has a sense of humor. He has to. He married me. I love to hear his stories of when he would go coon hunting and the pranks that he and his friends would pull on each other.

He is so much fun to scare. Just the other day, he had gone to sleep on the couch. I was in the bedroom and got up to go to the bathroom. He got up about the same time and entered the bathroom before I got there and didn't hear me come down the hall. I stood very still and waited until he came around the corner. All I said was "boo," but he did a silly little dance and grabbed me as if he was going to choke me. I cracked up! This is only about the one hundredth time I've scared him; but it's so much fun, and he reacts the same way every time.

Jim is much more than just my knight in shining armor. He is funny, full of life, and most of all, a wonderful, God-fearing Christian. The fact that he didn't try to kiss me the first time we were together is one thing, but most impressive is that he loves the Lord with all his heart and soul. I have seen him witness to others about the love of Jesus and pray without ceasing for people to come to the Lord. He loves to be around God's people and especially children.

I had already started working on the bus ministry with Gale Carpenter and had begun to work with Ed and Ruth Shanks in children's church. As the bus ministry grew, we began visitation on Saturday mornings to different neighborhoods. I was usually gone from eight to twelve every Saturday and would have to leave early to get on the bus to pick up the children on Sunday mornings. Jim drove me to catch the bus on Sundays, since we only had one car at the time. He really wasn't too thrilled about getting up earlier to do this and voiced it on more than one occasion.

One Sunday morning on the ride to catch the bus, he informed me he was going to another church that day. I had been praying that God would show him how much he needed to be involved with the bus ministry, but it just didn't seem like my prayers were being answered. When he announced he was going to another church, my heart was broken, and I told him, "Fine, if you don't care about these children and their souls, go right ahead!" I wanted so much for us to be in one accord and work together in the church. That morning during our time in children's church, someone came upstairs and told me that Jim was on the altar and that I needed to come downstairs. He told the church he had been convicted for several months to work with the bus ministry and with the children. He told them he had even thought about going to another church that morning just to get away from doing what

God wanted him to do. He still works in bus ministry today.

Hardly a Sunday went by that we didn't have one, two, or even three children home with us for Sunday dinner (I did eventually learn to cook). We were also still involved with the youth of the church and enjoyed singing with the choir. We were busy all through the week, going to work, church visitation, choir practice, bus ministry, children's church.

After a year, we bought our first home, a fixer-upper. I do mean *fixer-upper*. There was only one closet in the house. We had two bedrooms. If you were in the living room, then you only had to go a few steps to be in the bedroom. Our bedroom was so small that you had to crawl over the bed to make it up in the mornings. We painted, put down carpet, bought new appliances, fixed the porch, and called it home. Jim worked on the yard and cleared the little creek that ran along the house. Life was great. Our first little house was filled with love and the joy of serving Jesus. It is true. "All you need is love; love is all you need."

And He answered and said to them, "Have you not read that He who made them at the beginning '*made them male and female*,' and said, '*For this reason a man shall leave his father and mother and be joined to his wife, and the two shall become one flesh*'? So then, they are no longer two but one flesh. Therefore what God has joined together, let not man separate."

Matthew 19:4–6 (NKJV)

The Miracle of Birth

Jim and I always loved children and hoped and prayed that God would bless us with them when he felt it was the right time. We had been married about a year when I found out I was pregnant for the first time. We were so excited. I had not yet gone in for my first appointment when I first realized something was wrong. I began to have a little spotting and then it became more. I spoke with the doctor's office. They told me to rest, elevate my feet, and try not to worry. I was, of course, very worried and concerned. During the night, I began to cramp and bleed heavily. Jim was exhausted from working that day, so I tried to let him sleep as long as I could.

Finally, the pain was so unbearable that I had to wake him. We drove to the hospital, and later that afternoon, I had a miscarriage. We were heartbroken, but I was told this happened a lot in first pregnancies, and I had not been off birth control very long before becoming pregnant. All this seemed to make sense, and we decided to try again to have a child.

We conceived a second child. I was hesitant and worried, but once I got past the time that I had miscarried with the first child, I felt more at ease. Everything seemed to be going well. I had a baby shower. Everyone was so thrilled for us, especially at church. I worked at the Whiteway (a ten-cent store, for you older people; mini-Wal-Mart for the younger generation) but had decided to quit when the baby was due.

Toward the end of my pregnancy, I began to have some swelling and voiced my concern to the nurse, (the doctor did not see me each time). She explained that it was normal and I just needed to cut back on salt and drink more water. So I did. Three weeks later, I had gained thirty pounds. Now they were concerned and thought I must not have done what I was told—I had. My blood pressure was elevated. They immediately sent me to the hospital. I was told I had toxemia and was put on bed rest and assured that everything would be fine.

One morning, one of the doctors and a nurse came in the room and announced they were going to do an amniocentesis to see if the baby was big enough and the lungs developed enough to deliver. The procedure took place as they were telling me all of this. No X-rays were taken, and ultrasound had not yet been invented. My baby kicked once very hard after the procedure and did not move again. The next day a nurse from labor and delivery showed up and came to take the baby's heartbeat, but it was not found.

I began to panic and called Jim to come to the hospital. He had been in the room approximately five minutes when the doctor and several nurses surrounded my bed. The doctor listened for a heartbeat, propped his foot on the side of my bed, and announced that there had been fetal death. He proceeded to give me the reasons why the baby was dead: I didn't get enough rest, I had eaten salt, etc. I didn't hear a word except that my baby was dead. Labor was induced, and on October 20, 1975, James Hugh Manis, Jr. was carried into heaven by God's angels.

I felt as though someone had broken me in two. The day I came home was a beautiful fall day, and I remember telling Jim how beautiful a day it would have been to bring our son home and how I just wanted to go where he was. I couldn't understand why God had allowed this to happen. I was so hurt.

One of the hardest things was to go back to church and especially to work in children's church again, but I loved children. It eased my pain somewhat to try to bring them joy. One year passed, two years, three years. I had not become pregnant. I was actually afraid that I might become pregnant and endure the same heartache again. I changed gynecologists, and we discussed my trying to become pregnant again. He sent me to a heart specialist, and it was determined by both doctors that it was very risky for me to become pregnant again. My gynecologist suggested a tubal ligation procedure. Well, to me, this was the end. I would never be a mother—*never*. I tried to pray and could get no answer; not yes, not no, nothing. I guess sometimes we want God to talk to us in an audible voice, but most often he speaks to us in that still, small voice.

My surgery was to take approximately thirty minutes. It lasted one and a half hours. The first words my doctor said were, "Mrs. Manis, I don't see how you ever became pregnant to begin with. You probably would not have become pregnant again anyway." He told me that one tube was so damaged that it fell apart. They had burned, tied, and put little rings on my tubes to make sure of no further pregnancies, plus my tubes and ovaries did not connect to each other. I thought, *Okay,* this *is my answer from God.*

Jim and I had discussed adopting a baby. We felt now was the time to go forward with adoption procedures. We had interviews with the state adoption agency. They came to our home, talked with family and friends, took pictures of us. We even had separate interviews. I implored my neighbor to make tea when we had an interview at the house because mine wasn't very great. I wanted to make a good impression. Finally, all the interviews were over, and we were told the process took about a year before we received a bundle of joy.

Life was good again, and as is customary at our house on Halloween, I became a witch! It's true! Every year I dressed up and scared the children in the neighborhood when they came to trick or treat. Now, they always got a good scare and candy, but they also got a gospel tract. This year I just didn't feel very witchy. I felt as if I was coming down with a bug. After a few days, Jim suggested I go to my doctor. Were we in for a surprise! My doctor told me he thought I could be pregnant. I laughed. I said, "*Impossible.*"

He said, "I know. I did the procedure." After we both recovered from the shock, my doctor told me about all the risks of my being pregnant. *One:* it could be an ectopic pregnancy, which meant I could even possibly bleed to death if the tubes burst. *Two:* with the complications I'd had with the second pregnancy, I might again develop toxemia and could possibly die. He told me that there was also the option of an abortion to avoid a possible stroke or death.

All of this information was more than I could handle for one day. My doctor told me to go home and think about things, and we scheduled another appointment. I would do more than think; I would *pray.*

The next step was to tell Jim the news. He was ecstatic! Of course we were going to have this baby. Now that was an easy decision for him; it wasn't *his* body. Until you are face to face with a life-and-death decision like this, you really don't know what you will do. Although I already knew in my heart the decision I would make, I was afraid. I could not go through another pregnancy and another loss. I asked God's guidance and for faith in him to carry me through the next nine months.

When I returned for my appointment, I informed the doctor of my decision to go ahead with the pregnancy. I told him that even if it meant my life, I could not or would not end this baby's life. I was a Christian and did not believe in abortion. He said he knew me well enough to know what decision I was going to make even before I came back for the appointment. He promised to do everything he could to ensure this baby was born and we were both healthy.

The next months were hard. In April 1979, I had to be hospitalized because my blood pressure was elevated and my feet and hands were swollen. The baby was due on July 8, but on June 20, I went for my scheduled appointment and was immediately put in the hospital again. I had again developed toxemia. My heart sank. I cried on the way to the hospital. I could not believe I was going through this again.

Jim stayed with me that evening until about eight. I was restless and wide awake. Around eleven p.m. my water broke. A nurse from labor and delivery checked on the baby and me and said it still might be hours before the baby was born. I slept the rest of the night and called Jim the next morning. He was at the hospital in no time.

The morning wore on and still no baby and no labor pains. Since this was before ultrasound, the doctor decided an X-ray was needed to determine the baby's position. According to the doctor, the baby was in a difficult position. The head was bent back instead of forward. My pelvic bones were also somewhat fused, and I was not having any labor, and my uterus was heart shaped, which made for a harder delivery as well. He wanted to perform a C-section and asked if I would like to have my tubes removed. My immediate answer was no, and Jim's was yes. He said he would be back when we agreed one way or another. I had already made the decision once to have my tubes tied, and God had other plans. I would not make that decision again.

I felt God knew what he was doing (as always), and if a child was to be born to us, I didn't want to mess with anything.

I was prepped for a C-section, and on June 21, 1979, Julie Ann Manis cried for the first time. I think the whole room was in tears. I had never let myself believe I would hear a baby of my own cry, and I was overjoyed at the sound of her little voice even before I saw her. She was a tiny little bundle, five pounds, twelve ounces, with dark hair that stood straight up, ten little toes, and ten little fingers. She was perfect. God had blessed us after seven years of marriage with our own little miracle, and to this day I could never praise him enough.

There were some complications after the delivery. My blood pressure did not come down, and my body went into shock. I did not get to hold my little girl but for a minute. During the night, a nurse was stationed in the room with me to check on my blood pressure and vital signs. My doctor told me later that he had not expected me to live through the night because of the toxemia and blood pressure issues. But my God is good, and the next day I was holding my precious gift. We stayed in the hospital for another week while

I was given shots every three hours to lower my blood pressure.

We came home and there were twenty people at my house that night. Jim and I would just sit and stare at her. We watched every movement. *Look, she moved her fingers! Look, she made a face! Look—no, smell—she made a little poo-poo!* It was like having a *real* baby doll, and she was ours.

Time went on, and I could say life returned to normal; but it never did. Having a child changed our lives forever. We were excited to be parents, and every day seemed like a dream come true because we finally had a child.

Jim grew up with four sisters and a brother, and as I said earlier, I was an only child. We wanted to have another child, but since we did not know if that was possible, adoption became an option again. We prayed, and little Julie prayed as well. She told my mother we were praying about having a baby brother. It wasn't long before—you guessed it—I was pregnant again!

I seemed to do a lot better during this pregnancy, although I did throw up a lot more. Jim didn't even make it for this birth. I again had toxemia and was admitted to the hospital three or four days before the baby was born.

One evening, after Jim had left, I began to have some light labor. The nurses took me to labor and delivery and monitored the baby during the night. The next morning it was determined that another C-section was to be done. The nurses tried to reach Jim but could not. They had been dialing the wrong number. By the time he reached the hospital, it was all over. Julie had her little baby brother, and we had a precious little boy. James Elisha Manis was a short, chubby baby with blond hair.

My doctor decided to remove my tubes during the C-section. He said it was just too dangerous for my health to have another baby. He also added, "But with you, we never know."

Our family was complete. God had again blessed us beyond measure. I believe because we were faithful to God and told others how he had performed a miracle with the birth of our first child, he honored us with a second child. He tells us in his Word that he will give us the desires of our heart. Our desire was to serve him and to have children. What a wonderful God we serve!

Behold, children are a heritage from the Lord,
The fruit of the womb is a reward.

                                    Psalm 127:3 (NKJV)

A Mother's Hat (Chef, Coach, Hard Hat)

Don't get your Sunday clothes dirty. Sit up straight. Eat your peas, they're good for you (I hate peas). Say yes ma'am and no sir, please and thank you. Wash behind your ears and for heaven's sake, wear clean underwear if you're leaving the house.

These are some of the things we tell our children, but are they really *that* important? Now really, who's going to look behind your ears to see if they're clean?

Motherhood was and is certainly a challenge. Even though my children are grown and pretty much on their own, you never stop loving and caring about them, and you never stop being a mother. I will admit that I am not perfect (please don't tell my children) at being a mother. I've made my share of mistakes. That's for sure. Being a Christian mother is a joy, and every day is a blessing from God. Just think, as mothers, God has given us that wonderful privilege of molding our children into his image.

From the very beginning of their lives, Julie and Jimmy belonged to God, and I knew that he would have a special plan for them. The journey of their childhood and the lessons they learned have shaped them into the people they are today. I want to share some of that journey with you.

Julie has always been the independent child, the child who always asked, "Why, Mommy?" She was the reader and the tomboy. She had the most beautiful skin and dark eyes like her dad, and she was very petite. I dressed her in frilly dresses, but when she had the chance she wore blue jeans and a t-shirt and played ball or rode her bike. She loved her dolls and tried to mother Jimmy when he was little.

Julie was the child you had to keep an eye on or she wandered off to who knows where. One Saturday, I was working upstairs and Jim was working outside. He came upstairs and asked where Julie was.

I said, "With you."

"Oh no, she's not."

Thus began the hunt. We searched every nook and cranny in the house, upstairs and downstairs. After about ten minutes, Jim was in a panic. "Somebody has taken her! Call the police!"

My brother-in-law had also joined in the hunt, and guess what? He found her. She was hiding behind the basement stairs behind some boxes. She had been afraid to come out when she heard Jim yelling for her. She knew she was in trouble. He was so elated to find her that he didn't punish her but just squeezed her until she couldn't breathe.

Julie learned some of her lessons in stores. Once, when she was told to stay close by, she of course wandered away. I had told her what she was to do if we were ever separated in a store. I followed close behind yet out of sight to see if she would do what she had been told. She looked at the toys, the clothes for little girls, all the shiny stuff little girls liked. Then, all of a sudden, she realized that I wasn't where I had been and that she was lost. She went to the desk at the front of the store and promptly told the lady that her mommy was lost and could she please find her. I was right behind her. When we returned home, there was a long discussion about Mommy's getting lost. I promised to stay close to her the next time we went to the store, but she had to make sure that I did. She never got lost in the store again.

Another incident in a store happened when we had been shopping and I put the items and the children in the car. I noticed Julie had something shiny in her hands, and I inquired as to what it was. It was a pack of shiny sequins. I asked her where she got them, and she said she just picked them up. I thought this was a good time to teach her about taking things that didn't belong to us, so I took her back to the store and asked that we speak to the manager. He came to the front of the store. I made her hand over the sequins and apologize for taking them. I thought he would be kind and tell her he appreciated her honesty, but instead he gave her a look that even scared me and proceeded to tell her he could have her put in jail! She was only six or seven! I was irritated, but he let it go finally, and I took her to the car. She was visibly upset and in tears, but she never took anything from a store again.

Jimmy was our quiet child, at least most of the time. He was content just to sit and play with his Legos. He rarely got into trouble. He might fuss over putting up his toys, but he still did it. He liked playing outside, riding his bike, and playing with his beloved dog, Lucky.

Jimmy was afraid of dogs when he was small. We were visiting a friend, and a large collie puppy knocked him down. He wasn't hurt, but he had a fear of dogs after that. We decided the best way to get rid of that fear was to buy him a puppy. Lucky was a sheltie and loved Jimmy enormously. I never worried about Jimmy being out in the neighborhood because I knew Lucky was right beside him and watching out for him.

But Lucky couldn't help Jimmy on every occasion. We have some railroad ties at the bottom of our driveway, and one day Julie and Jimmy were playing on them. All of a sudden my mother and I heard bloodcurdling screams coming toward the house. Julie came running in, and Jimmy soon followed. He was so distraught he could hardly breathe. The words we heard were, "Somebody

MARCIA "CLEMENTINE" MANIS

help me, oh Lord, please help me. Somebody help me *please!*" He repeated this over and over. I didn't know if he was cut—I didn't see blood. I couldn't see anything visibly wrong! Julie tried to explain. "*Yellow jackets!*" were the only words she could say. Jimmy had borne the brunt of the yellow jackets' fury. He had been stung several times, and I guess he felt like he was still being stung. They must have had a nest in the railroad ties and become angry when the children jumped on them. It was so sad, yet when I think about it now, I can't help but giggle. The look on his face and those words; you would have thought the devil himself were after Jimmy.

Jimmy has always had a way of being comical even when he isn't trying. One day Julie and Jimmy came home from school on the bus. Julie rushed in and explained that Jimmy was in trouble, bad trouble. He had said a bad word on the bus and the bus driver had made him ride on the front seat. Jim questioned him to no avail. I told him I would try.

I took Jimmy into our bedroom, sat down in front of him, and asked him what he had said that was so bad. His reply was, "Are you gonna

82

whip me?" I had to think fast. I told him no, that I would never spank him for telling me the truth. Again he asked the same question, and again I told him the same answer. Finally, he decided to tell me what the word was. He immediately again asked if I was gonna whip him. I tried to contain my laughter and again told him I would not spank him for telling me the truth. However, punishment needed to be served for saying a bad word and getting in trouble on the bus. Jimmy loved to watch the *A-Team* on television. It was his favorite. I told him that for a week he could not watch the *A-Team*. I told him to tell his dad and then go to his room.

He marched straight to Jim and said, "I'm punished. I can't watch the *A-Team*," and went to his room. Now being the good Christian mother that I am, I thought this was an appropriate time to tell him that Jesus doesn't want us to say bad things and we should tell him we are sorry. He looked up at me with those little boy eyes and said, "Mom, he knows." That day Jimmy taught me a lesson as well. Jesus knows when we are truly sorry without us ever saying a word.

Jim and I also had another child we raised for

MARCIA "CLEMENTINE" MANIS

ten years. For privacy purposes, I will call her Dell. The important thing is that God knows her name. Dell and her Dad lived in a rundown motel on the edge of town. Jim started picking her up on the church bus on Sunday mornings, and she began to come home with us on Sunday afternoons. Her dad did his best for her, but it was soon apparent that he could not care for the needs of a little girl. Dell was eight years old yet still could not read or write well. We were told the Department of Human Services was going to step into the situation and she would be placed in foster care. Dell's dad asked if we would take care of her during the week and then let her stay with him on the weekends.

Julie was starting high school that year, and we had just repainted her room and added new things to reflect that she was now a teenager. Julie would have to share her new room with Dell because we only had three bedrooms. It was her decision whether Dell would live in our home.

Time was getting short before school started, and I knew I had to come up with an alternative plan if Julie decided she did not want Dell to share her room.

Dell was not always clean or well groomed when she stayed with her dad. I didn't want children to make fun of her at school because of the way she looked. Even though I might not be there to bathe her and fix her hair, I wanted her clothes to be clean and fresh. I ironed five little outfits, pinned clean underwear and socks to them, and numbered them one to five. She didn't know the days of the week, but I knew she could count, and that would assure that she had clean clothes every day. While I was ironing the clothes downstairs, Julie came in and looked at me and said, "Mom, it's okay. Dell can share my room." I admired her willingness to give and to love someone she didn't know. That was the day my Julie became a young woman.

Dell was a challenge. For one thing, I couldn't believe I had agreed to take on an eight-year-old. I was getting old! She exhausted me. Dell was not used to discipline, and every day became a battle. Finally, I was at wits' end! One day I chased her through the house, and she had landed on my bed, jumping up and down on it and screaming to the top of her lungs that she didn't have to do anything I told her. That was it. I smacked her bottom and sent her to her room. She was startled. I don't think she had ever had a spanking before. That night, when we were saying our prayers, she said all the God blesses, and for the first time I was included in them. I wasn't sure if she wanted God to bless me so I wouldn't spank her again or if she was glad that I had shown her enough love to spank her.

Dell grew and learned a lot of things while she lived with us. When she first came to live with us she was shy and would hide behind me. Eventually, she learned to be part of a group and overcame the shyness. The first time we took her to the beach she developed a sunburn. You would have thought she was going to die. We got through that okay too.

One of the trials for Dell was how to eat good food. She was used to eating a hamburger from McDonald's or eating food straight from a can. She didn't like vegetables or different meats. Usually after every dinner, she made herself throw up. She was going to show us that she didn't have to eat what was prepared for her. One day she threw up on the kitchen floor. I made her clean it up. No more throw up after that.

We eventually fixed up a room downstairs for

Dell. We wallpapered and painted, got a new bed-spread for her bed, and made curtains for her window. She had her own television, VCR, and stereo. She had toys, Barbie dolls, and a bike; everything a little girl could want.

Dell had a struggle in school. Studying was difficult, and I made every effort to go to the school every year and make sure she got the extra help she needed. Julie had always pushed herself in school and made very good grades. Jimmy struggled and was diagnosed with ADD when he was in the fifth grade. Dell always felt that we thought she could not live up to Julie and Jimmy. We told her that we just wanted her to do the best she could do, and I always knew she had the potential to do more. She didn't believe us.

Jim and I tried to love her as our own. I know there were perhaps times when she did not feel as though she was part of our family, but we did the best we could. The week after her eighteenth birthday, she left a note for us while I was gone shopping. She had decided to move in with her boyfriend and his family. We tried over and over to convince her to come home. Nothing worked. I felt as though I had failed as her mother. We were

87

robbed of enjoying her senior prom, her graduation, and eventually her wedding to her boyfriend. At the writing of this book, she is divorced and trying to raise a child on her own.

On numerous occasions since Dell left our home, I have heard the story of the prodigal son. One specific Sunday, something was said I had just not grasped before. The son had to come home to the father; the father didn't go to the son. I know that one day, Dell will come home to us and to her heavenly Father. She professed her faith as a Christian, and I pray every day that she will find her way back to him.

When my children were young, I could kiss their boo-boos and love away their fears. As they grew older, it wasn't that easy. Their feelings were hurt with an unkind word, or maybe they didn't get the grade they worked so hard for on a test. During those times, the hat of motherhood was hard to wear. I tried to comfort them. I told them how Jesus wanted them to behave and hoped they listened.

I think the teenage years are by far the hardest for children and mothers. For one thing, we become totally stupid in their eyes. We know nothing about how to choose the right friends, the new hairstyles, or the latest fashion in clothes. We're just not cool.

Eventually, you do become intelligent, usually their first or second year in college. I have never regretted having children, even though many times the road was rocky and filled with potholes. I love my children and will love them until I draw my last breath.

///

Train up a child in the way he should go, And when he is old he will not depart from it.

Proverbs 22:6 (NKJV)

My first bonnet!

Curls and Crinolines

Dad, Grandmother Price, Doris and me

Grandmother Price, her pipe and her dog

Easter bonnets and corsages–all decked out

Oh where have you been darling Billy? BIG BONNET!

"Clowning" in the ocean

My last birthday with Dad-My sweet sixteen

My Graduation

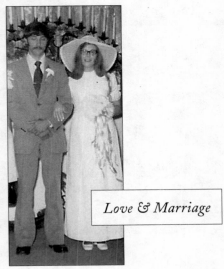

Love & Marriage

Sadness

Julie's car accidednt

Noah

Annie & Abbie

Clementine

Pearl

Gertrude Gossip

Beatrice Bumble Boufant

Lanelle Dubois

*Hazel Hildebrand
Humperdink*

Nurse I. V. Needles

Lillie

The family

Jimmy & Sabrina

Jim, Julie, Shannon, Garrett, Alan, Renee and Me

Nose to Nose!

Clown Chapeaux

A true clown has a serious heart condition for which there is no cure. Countless studies, X-rays, and CT scans have been done but to no avail. It's not easy living with this condition, and while there is no cure, it is a condition the patient is able to maintain and manage for his entire life. It is called L.A.U.G.H.T.E.R. for short and stands for Love And Understanding, Grace, Happiness, Tickles, and Eternal Rejoicing.

I noticed this condition in others at a very young age. The clowns I saw at the Shrine Circus with my dad made me laugh. They wore strange, bright clothing, red noses, and funny hats. I began to develop the condition myself at that very moment. Later, in my early teenage years, I dressed up as Raggedy Ann with pigtails and glued patches of material on my cheeks and a red nose. The condition had worsened.

I had a period of remission, and then one year in Vacation Bible School, I entered into a place of no return. I led the music for Bible School and felt like the kids would really enjoy something different in the middle of the week. I sewed up a clown jumpsuit, red on one side and polka dots on the other. I bought a rainbow-colored wig at K-Mart and found makeup at a tuxedo rental store. I was ready. Now what about a name? Well, this clown, of course, was a Christian, so what about Clementine, the Christian clown? It seemed to fit. The children were so excited and I knew that I had found my true calling.

For years, Clementine showed up at Bible school while the music leader was nowhere to be found. Then one day, I was approached about our church starting a clown ministry. Since I was usually the only official clown at church, I agreed. We attended a Christian clown mini-conference in Covington, Georgia, and then later in the year, I went to a week-long conference at the Georgia Baptist Assembly in Taccoa, Georgia, called TNT (Teaching and Training for Jesus). I could not believe it. There were clowns from all over the country—New York, Minnesota, and California. There was even one from Iceland!

The conference was like a school, revival, and homecoming all wrapped into one. I learned so much that first year, like how to apply makeup correctly, the proper wig and how to care for it, gospel illusions, face painting, balloon animals (not my thing—my poodle looked like a blue-tick hound). The list is endless, and there was never enough time to take all the classes that were offered. I have gone back to TNT every year since the first conference to learn more and more. Each year is filled with new classes and wonderful leaders, but the most important thing I come away with every year is the revival in my soul to spread the gospel of Jesus to others. Who knew that a clown could share Jesus in such a wonderful way!

A clown is sometimes more easily approachable than a preacher in a suit, especially by children. Each time I sit down to paint a child's face, the opportunity is there to share the gospel, to hand out a gospel tract and sticker, and to see a smile appear on that child's face. Nothing is more rewarding or blesses my soul more than to make

MARCIA "CLEMENTINE" MANIS

a child happy. I believe that clown ministry is a seed-planting ministry. We plant the seeds of sharing the gospel, but someone else will water that seed, and someone else will see that seed blossom into a beautiful Christian.

It always makes my heart rejoice when I know that God is using my clown character to show his love. I have had children run up to me in the mall just to give the clown a hug. At other times, the language barrier has been broken by placing a red nose sticker on a face and handing out a gospel tract in Spanish. Clowns have no nationality. They are just clowns.

Reverend Buddy Lamb has been the camp chaplain at TNT for several years and is the pastor of Schomburg Road Baptist Church in Georgia. His phrase, "Clowning is more than an art form; it's a heart form," is so true. You can't be a Christian clown unless you know Jesus as your personal savior, and then clowning is not just fun or art—it truly is a heart form. In the introduction to Buddy's book, *Clown Scripts for Churches*, there is a section that gives five points on how a clown can bless. The first is a meaningful touch (a caring touch); the second, a spoken word; the third, attaching great worth to what we do and say as Christian clowns (in other words, "Oh be careful little tongue, what you say"); the fourth is instilling hope—hope that takes them away from the problems of life and leads them to Christ, who has hope; and the fifth, to have an active commitment, Christian clowns must be committed to their calling, use their talent to bless the people they are reaching out to, and to reach those hearts for Jesus.

Clowns are often described as entertainers in the church. That's correct; we are. According to Buddy Lamb and to Webster's Dictionary, the word *entertain* means to keep, hold, or maintain in the mind, or to receive and take into consideration. Why wouldn't we as clowns want to keep, hold, maintain in the mind, and let the audience receive and take into consideration the blood of the Lamb and his sacrifice for our sins? Wouldn't it be wonderful if we entertained the whole world into heaven?

My journey as a clown started with Clementine, but it didn't end there! Before I knew it, different characters began to emerge. A lot of them started out with hats. As I have said before, I love hats. A hat conveys who you are. If you are a chef, you wear a chef's hat; a fireman, a fireman's hat; a policeman, a policeman's hat. You are often identified by the hat you wear.

One of the first characters the Lord developed for me was a lady named Gertrude Gossip. I had been shopping with my daughter to find a dress for Christmas. Julie tried on at least a half dozen dresses, and I began to get bored. How hard can it be to find a dress when you wear a size five? We happened to be close to the hat rack, and I began to try some of them on. I knew this would draw attention and that Julie would be embarrassed and pick out the dress, and we could go home.

A certain hat caught my eye. It was bright red felt with a huge red bow perched on one side. I loved it, but I wasn't willing to pay full price for it! We went home, but I couldn't get that hat off my mind, and a character to fit the hat immediately came to my mind. I went back several weeks later during the after-Christmas sale, and the hat was 50 percent off. What a bargain! I bought it. The rest of Gertrude's wardrobe came together. She is a gossip columnist for the local paper and came to church one Sunday to pick up on the latest news. Where else can you find such juicy gossip?

There are other characters. There is Nurse IV Needles, Bug-Eyed Betsy Brown, Sally McSparkle, Mrs. Claus, Pearl, Betty Sue Bop, Hazel Hildebrand Humperdink. Each character is unique and each wears a different hat, but each character tells the story of Jesus and how much he loved us and died for us.

Nurse IV Needles is a very special character who visits the hospitals, nursing homes, and retirement homes. Her presence brings a smile to those who feel alone or scared. Simple things like blowing bubbles and spinning plates or getting a sticker to put on the bulletin board makes a frown turn upside down.

I cannot begin to tell you how the Lord has blessed me in this wonderful ministry. Different characters have appeared at ladies' conferences, Sunday schools, community events, and churches. They have brought cheer and a message of hope and love about Jesus and have drawn me closer to him.

I believe that God wants us to show the joy he has given us through his son, Jesus. We need to lift up the fallen and the brokenhearted and not only tell them about the love of Jesus but let them see the joy that he brings to each life that seeks after him. The best day in my life was when I became a Christian.

The little song, "Running over, running over, my cup is full and running over; since the Lord saved me, I'm as happy as can be. My cup is full and running over," describes how we as Christians should feel about telling others about him. Our cups should be so full of God's love that we can't wait to share it! I am amazed God has used my talent in such a wonderful and special way.

I love being a clown and have made lifelong friends with other clowns. It is a blessing to hear that others are sharing Jesus in this unique way. Clowning may not seem like much of a ministry to a lot of people, but as this song says, "Little is much when God is in it; Labor not for wealth or fame. There's a crown, and you can win it, if you go in Jesus' name."

If we are willing and available to God, he will direct our paths and use the talents we possess for his glory. You may think your talent is small and God can't use you for his work, but he used little David in a great way, and he can use you no matter what your talent may be.

A Clown's Prayer:

As I stumble through this life, help me to create more laughter than tears, dispense more cheer than gloom, spread more cheer than despair.

Never let me become so indifferent that I will fail to see the wonders in the eyes of a child or the twinkle in the eyes of the aged.

Never let me forget that my total effort is to cheer people, make them happy, and help them forget momentarily all the unpleasantness in their lives.

And in my final moment, may I hear you whisper: "When you made my people smile, you made me smile."

-Anonymous-

Worst Hat I Ever Had to Wear

The spring of 1996 was a wonderful time of year. I had started a new job in January. Julie, Jimmy, and Dell were doing well in school, and Jim was hard at work as usual.

Julie has always been the athletic child in the family. She played softball and ran track, and that year she decided that she wanted to try out for a cheerleading position. I remember her coming in from school so excited. She had made the squad; however, she was also the most accident-prone child I had. She could find the same hole in the yard (and did) and fall in it numerous times (sprained ankles). Her legs always looked like we had beaten her from the bruises and abrasions

MARCIA "CLEMENTINE" MANIS

she sustained from her adventures. She decided one day that it would be grand if she and Jimmy took a ride in her wagon down the hill in front of our house. Wagons don't have brakes. She landed at the bottom of the hill, face first, with Jimmy perched on top of her. Jim came running through the house with Julie in his arms and exclaimed there had been an accident. I thought someone had hit them with a car! All I could see was blood on Julie's face. I asked where Jimmy was. "He's coming," was the reply. He didn't even have a scratch. Julie, on the other hand, had screamed when she went flying through the air and landed with a mouth full of gravel. I took her to the emergency room to check for fractures. She had none and thought the coolest thing was being able to see her elephant earrings on the X-ray.

Another time, she decided she could ride on the back of a four-wheeler. She knew she wasn't allowed to ride one, much less be on the back of one. It flipped and ran over her. She came limping to the house and tried to convince us that she was just standing there and it fell on top of her. Jim, who was on the phone and immediately hung up, told her he knew better. She had tire marks on her leg and black dirt and grit in her hair. Again, another trip to the emergency room to make sure her leg wasn't broken. It wasn't, but she was grounded for two weeks.

Still another time, she fell down the basement stairs. The list could go on forever. I'm truly surprised that she never broke a bone; usually only her pride was broken.

The accident I will never forget happened on Saturday, May 18, 1996. The youth were having a car wash at the church. Julie and Jimmy had taken our Ford Aerostar van to get a thorough cleaning but were to return at lunchtime so I could run some errands. Julie showed up without Jimmy. Instead, three of her girlfriends were with her. I was not pleased and told her I was concerned that the girls' parents might not want them to be with a young driver. She assured me that it was all right and that she would run the errand I needed and take Jimmy's lunch to him. I relented and told her I loved her, to be careful, and to fasten her seatbelt. I proceeded to take a shower, and within five minutes the phone was ringing. One of the girls was on the phone and calmly told me there had been an accident. I asked if everyone was okay, and she said no. I didn't ask who was hurt, but because she was so calm, I thought it could only be a little fender-bender. I told her I'd be there as soon as possible. My neighbor drove me to the accident.

The first image I saw was that of fire trucks; the next was a Camaro sideways in the road and next to a tree. When I topped the hill, I saw the worst thing I could possibly imagine. My van was upside down, the driver's door ripped off, the left wheel and axle lying in the road, a helicopter landing, and my precious daughter lying on a stretcher and covered in blood from head to toe. All I could say over and over was, "Oh no, Julie, oh no!"

She tried to comfort me and tell me everything was okay. When I saw a gaping hole in her right shoulder and the amount of blood she was losing, I knew it wasn't okay. I grabbed one of the paramedics and begged him to tell me how bad it was. He said she had lost a lot of blood, but he thought she would be okay, and then he walked away. I knew he walked away because he couldn't tell me the truth. Jim was at work, and I noticed the phone hanging from the car and called him with the news. I told him Julie had had an accident and to come to the scene. I wasn't sure what hospital they were taking her to. He was so distraught that he just left work and drove his truck to the local hospital. He didn't even remember which child I had said was hurt or that they were flying her to a hospital. When he arrived at the local hospital, the other girls were there, and he was assured they were only shaken and scratched up. He finally came to the scene, and when he saw the van, he broke down in tears.

While I was waiting for Jim to get to the van, which seemed an eternity, a man approached me and asked if I was a Christian. I said yes, and he asked if he could pray with me. I told him by all means, let us pray. I did not know at the time that he was a local pastor and had happened on the scene.

There were a lot of things that *just happened* that day. The helicopter *just happened* to be at the local park for Meet Your Rescuer Day. I *just happened* to get Julie the bag cell phone five months earlier because I was concerned she might be on the road and need it someday. Our friend *just happened* to be walking in her yard and hear the wreck that day and call the rescue squad. The girls in the van *just happened* to stay calm and call 911 and their parents from the phone in the van. God *just happened* to be right there. I don't think so. God knew all along what would happen that day, and he was there every step of the way.

Friends drove us to the hospital thirty miles away where they had airlifted Julie, and though we were going around ninety miles per hour, I felt we were moving at a snail's pace. I had the sinking feeling Julie would be gone when we arrived. We finally drove up to the emergency room and were directed to go the waiting area. Julie was having a CT scan and X-rays to check for broken bones, etc.

When we were finally allowed to see her in the emergency room, I wanted to scream. Jim broke down and cried, and Julie again assured us that she was all right. The left side of her face was torn away and exposed her jaw bone; her left ear was almost torn away. On her left arm, large chunks of her skin were missing, and her right shoulder had a hole large enough to stick your fist in and spread your hand apart.

Julie was taken to surgery, and we waited for what again seemed an eternity. While she was in surgery, the details of the crash came to light. The road the accident happened on is very narrow. Our van was large, and because the road was so narrow, you almost had to ride the ditch line to stay in the correct lane. They were coming up on a curve when the Camaro came around the curve and hit them driver's side head on. The van catapulted over the Camaro and landed upside down. The door was ripped off, and the van slid with Julie hanging out the open door. She had seen the wreck coming and had reached her left arm across her face and had her right arm extended to catch the girl in the passenger seat. To my knowledge, Julie was the only one in the car wearing a seatbelt. When the van landed, the girls saw her lying on the ground in a pool of blood. They thought she was dead, and then she moaned. They told her to get up and helped her to the other side of the car, where she sat on the ground. They were wearing bathing suits and removed their t-shirts to try and stop the bleeding. Glass and the pavement caused the injury to her face and left arm, and a piece of metal from the inside top of the van caused the injury to her right shoulder and breast.

The night of Julie's surgery, she was listed in critical condition and taken to a step-down unit.

We were told to stay with her and help watch her airway. Her face and neck were swollen, and she had a concussion. She never opened her eyes, but she would talk to us. I told her that everyone was praying for her, and she replied that she had prayed in the helicopter on the way to the hospital. I asked what she had prayed, and she said she had asked God to take care of her. I told her he had.

I could not sleep, but Jim was exhausted and went to sleep in the chair. The same was true for the second night—no sleep for me and no peace. I felt that if I went to sleep, Julie would need me and I wouldn't be able to respond. On Monday, she was moved to the rehabilitation part of the hospital. By now her face was so swollen that her eyes were almost shut, and she was bruised and in a great deal of pain. We went down to physical therapy, and for the first time I saw the true extent of her injuries. When they were lowering her into a whirlpool bath, I was asked if I wanted to stay. I told them of course, I was her mother. Where else would I be? I was told no one usually stayed. I soon understood why. Julie was in so much pain that she screamed and cried as I held her hand.

She had so many open wounds, and they were so deep. I can't imagine the agony she was in.

On the way back to the room, my heart felt as if it would burst. Why hadn't I been the one in the car? Why hadn't I taken them back to church? How could I make this better? So many questions and no answers. I was her mother, and I couldn't fix this. I told Jim it would never be better and I didn't know what to do.

By this time we were all exhausted. Jim had gone home to rest the day before, but I still could not sleep and would not leave Julie. I sat in a reclining chair next to her bed. I had not been able to pray. My mind would not let me. I asked the Lord to let me rest and be strong so that I could take care of my child. I asked him to heal her broken body and restore her health. He answered my prayer for rest, and I slept.

We soon fell into a routine for each day. A small breakfast and pain medication to help her relax in the whirlpool was first on the agenda. We would have prayer together every morning and ask God to get her through the day. All of the nurses were wonderful, especially the ladies in physical therapy. They were both Christians, and

I felt blessed that they cared so much about their patients and especially Julie. The reality of what had happened soon set in, and there were days that Julie was so depressed and down. When she was a little girl I had always told her, *pretty is as pretty does.* I would try to comfort her and tell her she was a beautiful person on the inside as well as on the outside. There were many days that she did not believe me.

One of the things that truly amazed me was the outpouring of love and concern from so many people. There was a waiting room across from Julie's room. Most of the time, it was full of her friends from school, our church family, and relatives. On the Sunday after the accident, people had been turned away because of the overflow of visitors. Everyone found out that Julie liked bears, and before long her room looked more like the gift shop than a hospital room. Others found out she had trouble eating and needed to gain some weight before they did skin grafts on her shoulder. We were flooded with food: mashed taters, donuts, taco bell, and her favorite, Reese's Peanut Butter Cup ice cream.

There are many other things I could tell you

about Julie's days in the hospital, but the most important thing is the good that came from all the tragedy. As a Christian parent you try to teach your children to follow the Lord, stand up for what is right, and let God lead their lives. You don't know how they are really affecting other lives because you aren't with them each hour of the day. Julie belonged to the Lord even before she was born, and when she was born we gave her back to him and thanked him for the blessing of getting to be the parents who would mold her in his image. The teenagers who came to see her told us they knew she was a Christian by the way she lived her life. They could not understand why she had to suffer. I am sure Mary wondered the same thing when Jesus was suffering on the cross. She was his mother, and her heart broke as well to see the pain he must endure for our sins.

Julie was probably the strongest, both physically and spiritually, of the girls in the car accident. Jennifer Linkous was one of the girls in the car that day. I worked with her mother at the Health Department, and she had told me that Jennifer was not saved. Jennifer had not really participated with the youth a great deal, and I suggested to

Julie that she take her under her wing and become her friend. Jennifer went on a youth trip with us, and we talked about her salvation, but she still did not accept Jesus.

The day of the accident, I had told Julie to ask Jennifer if they could sit together at church on Sunday. I told her that all Jennifer probably needed was a friend to walk with her down the aisle of the church and make a decision for Christ. We knew Jesus was dealing with her heart. The morning following the accident, Jennifer gave her heart and life to Jesus.

I don't know why my daughter had a horrible accident and suffered so much. What I do know is that I serve a marvelous Savior who can see beyond the hurt and the pain and can heal our bodies and give us strength to live another day for him. So many good things came from the accident that day. A soul was saved. We were shown tremendous love—from strangers, from God's people, and the unfailing love of God.

Without God's sustaining strength, Julie could not have endured. She has been strong in her faith for him. Julie has undergone more than ten other surgeries since the accident and has grown stronger physically and spiritually. She went on to be a cheerleader, even though she was in pain. She graduated from high school with honors and eventually graduated from college summa cum laude with a master's in education. She is a teacher and married to a wonderful Christian man, Shannon Smith. She will soon give birth to our second grandchild.

Many people encouraged and took care of my needs as well. One particular friend knew I drank hot tea and brought a box of scripture tea to the hospital. The following scripture blessed my heart during Julie's recovery and gave me strength to help my child through difficult days. My desire was to see my child healthy. Not only has God given me the desires of my heart, but he has blessed me beyond measure.

//

Delight yourself also in the Lord, and He shall give you the desires of your heart.

Psalm 37:4 (NKJV)

A Veil of Tears

It seems like trouble always comes in threes or maybe fours. Of course, God did not promise us that life would be easy. Even among the beautiful roses, there are thorns.

The years following Julie's car accident were filled with more surgeries, getting her ready for college, Dell reaching puberty, and Jimmy getting a driver's license. If that isn't enough to drive you crazy, there is more.

My mother had lived on her own since I married, and even though she did not drive, she managed her household well. She lived about five miles from us, and because she had supportive and caring neighbors, I knew that when we could not be there, they would watch out for her. When I could not go by and check on Mom, Jim would stop by after work to check on her. She loved Julie and Jimmy, and they would get off the bus after school at her house.

Not long before Julie's accident, I noticed a change in my mother. I would tell her something, and she would swear I had never told her anything about whatever it was. Many times she would get angry, and there were times she didn't speak to me for days because of something she thought I had said or not said. Her physical health was beginning to decline as well, and finally after she was hospitalized twice at the beginning of 1998, I convinced her to sell her house and move in with us. One of her doctors diagnosed her with Alzheimer's, and I knew she could no longer live alone. She was never told.

It was another change for the children. Jim's parents had lived with us for a short time before this, and we had rearranged rooms for everyone to sleep in. Jimmy seemed to get the short end of the stick. He slept on the couch. Now again, Mother was taking over his room, and he was again on the couch. He never complained.

Even though my mother had the early stages of Alzheimer's, it did not deter her from being a perfectionist. Her home was always immaculate, dinners perfect. I can't even remember her burning anything! Well, this perfectionism came into play when we began to build an apartment for her onto our home. I was still working full time when we started building in May. We hired someone to build the apartment, but to save some money, Jim and I worked in the evenings doing clean-up work, staining doors, painting, and other odd jobs. My Saturdays were spent taking Mother to buy materials, appliances, paint, and wallpaper. The apartment was finished by Labor Day. Mother seemed satisfied with the apartment, although I am sure she was never as happy as she had been living in her own home. She could still take care of most of her cleaning, and since she still had a working kitchen (which she had insisted on), she did most of her cooking. I did her laundry and cleaned the floors for her. I did not want her to think we were completely taking over.

My mother was the youngest in her family, the baby girl, and I believe the most petted. I know that my dad spoiled her. He didn't want his wife to work outside the home, so my mother was a home-maker. He showered her with love and attention.

She prided herself on her home and how well she took care of things. But when Daddy died at such a young age, she was not prepared. She had never taken care of the bills or driven a car. Her world changed just as mine had. I became the source of income after we moved to Tennessee until she was able to draw a pension.

My mother had always brought me up in church, but as years passed, she changed. She had been a Sunday school teacher, Vacation Bible School teacher, and a Girls Auxiliary leader while I was growing up. When I left home and married, for a few years she dated again. When that did not work out and the man she dated married someone else, she became bitter. She no longer came to church, and I could not speak to her about it. She only got angry and told me she could worship God at home just as well as at church. I guess she had to blame someone for the anger and hurt she felt, and I often bore the brunt of that anger.

Jim and I took her most of the places she wanted to go. We always took her on vacations with us and tried to include her in anything we did. But many times I would hear her tell people, "Well, if I only had a way." I could scream.

We were the way, and if she asked, we took her. She also had disapproved, and for what reason I was never quite sure, of Dell being in our family. On almost every occasion that I spoke with her, she reminded me that she was not Dell's grandmother. I don't know if she was jealous that we had one more child to take care of and it meant less time spent with her. I just don't know.

In December of 1998 I was laid off from my job and began baby-sitting for Noah (you'll hear more about him later). My days fell into a routine. I took care of Noah, who was a toddler, checked on Mom, did laundry, ran errands, and cooked supper. I tried to take care of everyone's needs. Remember, I had a child in college and two teenagers, and oh yes, a husband! A lot of times I felt as though I was spread very thin (although my body didn't get any thinner).

Jimmy was a junior in high school and dating. He had always been pretty trustworthy and honest with us. He seemed to have a good head on his shoulders, and he knew the boundaries we set for him. Our children did not *lay out* of church. If the doors were open, they were there. They may not like it, but that's just the way it was going to be.

Jimmy's grades began to falter, and we found out he had skipped some school. I found marijuana in his pocket one night, and he came up with the excuse that someone had planted it. I believed it because I wanted to. I had too much on my mind. I wanted to believe this son who had never been in any trouble, but I wondered if he wasn't running around with the wrong kind of people at school. I prayed. Another time, I knew he had been drinking when he came in late. Again I prayed and asked God to turn his life around.

During this time, my mother's condition worsened. She began putting her bills in her underwear drawer and grew angrier each day. She had even told people we were taking her money and not buying her groceries. (Not true.) I was now fixing her lunch and supper.

In October of 1999, I was sitting at the kitchen table and heard my mother scream from her apartment. I found her slumped down at the end of her bed. I had no idea what happened, but she told me she could not walk. Jim and I managed to get her to a chair. I asked her if she fell. She didn't know. I feared she had broken a hip, so we rushed her to the emergency room. The X-rays showed no broken bones, but she could not remember what day it was, who was president, or even her birthday. She was hospitalized for a week. Again the answer was Alzheimer's. For whatever reason, sometimes Alzheimer's patients tend to take a turn for the worse. This was Mom's worse.

She knew us, or at least seemed to know us. She became convinced that Jimmy had been killed in a car accident and that we were not telling her anything about it. She insisted over and over that we tell her the arrangements of the funeral. We could not convince her he was fine, even when my brother-in-law brought him to the hospital and she saw him with her own eyes. She spoke to him and then turned to me and asked again when the funeral was going to be. She kept me awake for several nights until her mind finally settled.

We arranged for a hospital bed to be put in Mom's apartment when she came home. I slept in her bedroom during the week, and Jim and the children took turns on the weekends. She rarely left that bed. I tried to encourage her to watch television or read. She would not. She only stared at the ceiling. God only knows what went on in her mind. She became less angry and more complacent. She did not sleep at night and constantly hollered my name for one reason or another. There were times when Mother's mind was better than others, and I did have some help from a home health agency for her bathing and physical therapy.

I still tried to keep going to church during this time. It was my strength, even though I rarely got to hear any preaching. Just being with God's people and with the children at church helped me get through the week ahead. We never left Mother alone, so we worked out a schedule. Jim would run the church bus and come home, and I would go for Children at Worship or choir practice. I would leave a few minutes early, and he came back to church in time to take people home. It wasn't ideal, but it worked. I cannot thank God enough for my family during this time. Jim and the children helped out in any way they could.

One Friday night in February 2000, Mother had again kept me up, and Noah had begged to spend the night. I finally got them settled and was waiting for Jimmy to come home. One of his friends was to spend the night. He came home all right—drunk! I had had it. You could see it in his eyes. Tonight's story was that someone had given them the beer. They were underage, someone handed it to them in a parking lot, and of course they drank it. I asked Jimmy if he was driving. He said yes. I asked the other boy if he had been drinking. "Oh no," was the reply. I knew better, but I told him he wasn't much of a friend to let Jimmy drink and drive. I was so furious.

I loaded them in the car, ranted and raved all the way to the boy's house, and dropped him off. The more I thought about it, the madder I got. Mad at Jimmy, but mostly mad at the devil. I was determined he would not have my son. This child was the Lord's whether he wanted to be or not. I told Jimmy we were going directly to the police station, and he could tell them his story about someone giving him beer. He cried, begged, and pleaded, but I refused to hear any of it. I wanted to at least scare him to death and let them tell him what the consequences were if he were caught drinking and driving before he turned eighteen. The officer informed him we would have an option to leave him in jail or not. I let him know spending the night in jail was the only option! I think by the time we left, he knew his mother had reached her tolerance level, even though she loved him with all her heart.

I was exhausted when we returned home at two a.m. I fell asleep. Mother woke me bright and early. I fixed her breakfast, crushed and dispensed her meds, and bathed her for the day. I had a splitting headache and told her I was going to lie down for a little while. She knew the monitor was on so I would be able to hear her if she needed me. Jim and Jimmy had left for town, Dell was at a neighbor's, and Julie was working. I had just fallen into a good sleep when Jim woke me up and told me that something was wrong with Mother. He and Jimmy had never left. She had called them to come back in the room and help her to the bathroom. I had just taken her before I went to sleep and thought maybe she just wanted some attention.

She seemed to be hyperventilating and had done this before, so I tried to get her to slow her breathing and then take a sip of water. It did not help. We decided to get her back to bed. She slumped down in the doorway of the bathroom, and Jim caught her. As he was walking her back to the bed, I knew something was terribly wrong.

Her face was whiter than a sheet, and her breathing was not good. I dialed 911, but I knew by the time we got her back to bed that she was gone. They insisted that we start CPR, and Jim tried but was so upset that he wasn't sure if he was doing it correctly. Jimmy had just taken a course at school and told Jim he knew how to do it. He asked Jimmy to take over, and Jimmy burst into tears and said he didn't think he could. Jim told him that he had to do it, and Jimmy did the best he could, but she was already dead.

Even though my heart was sad because my mother had died, my concern was immediately turned to Jimmy. I did not want him to blame himself because he could not save her or because he was not where God wanted him to be in his life when she died. He spoke very little during the next few days. I could tell his heart was broken.

A few months passed, and Jimmy graduated in May of that same year. I did not see a great change in his life. I prayed. The youth of our church were to participate in Pathfinders, a Scott Dawson ministry that teaches teenagers how to witness to others and allows them to do just that during a week-long conference. After witnessing and handing out flyers during the day, they converge at night for praise and worship and a message from Scott Dawson. Jim and I were traveling to Indiana for my thirty-year reunion, and Jimmy was to attend this conference. However, he had decided on a different plan: party hardy while we were gone. The girl he was dating at the time also belonged to the youth group, and after much pleading from her, Jimmy agreed to attend the conference with her. I am so thankful he did.

We returned home to find a different Jimmy. A son who stopped me in the kitchen one day and told me he felt God was doing something in his life, but he did not know what. He further explained that one night during the Pathfinders conference he had felt as though the preacher were speaking directly to him. He was searching to fill the void in his life that alcohol and drugs would never fill. He went to the altar and completely turned his life over to God. A year later, Jimmy answered the Lord's call to become a minister.

The words on the pages of this chapter of my life did not take long to write, but the tears, pain, and struggle took years. Those years have been spent in prayer and searching for answers to come to a peace about my mother. At forty-eight, I felt abandoned and alone with no parents, and I wasn't even sure how my mother had really felt about me. She had rarely shown any real affection for me in so many years. I could not believe that a mother could say and do such hurtful things. But my Father God is a great healer of hearts, and I have made peace with the past.

God is always faithful and has proven it in my life time and time again. He heals broken hearts and restores lives. He restored my son to a right fellowship with him, and now he tells the world about Jesus. No matter where Jimmy is, he is not ashamed of the gospel of Jesus Christ. I know God is going to use him in a great and mighty way. He is currently a part-time youth minister and full-time student. He has been on foreign mission trips and will be leaving again this year for Africa.

I know the power of prayer works because I see it every day in my own life. If we are not going through a trial, we soon will. Our trials can either break us or make us lean on Jesus. I am so thankful that his shoulders are broad and that I can lean on them at any time, safe and secure from all alarms.

I can come through the trials of a long night, lean on everlasting arms, and have joy in the morning.

//

Come to Me, all you who labor and are heavy laden, and I will give you rest.

Matthew 11:28 (NKJV)

Weeping may endure for a night, but joy comes in the morning.

Psalm 30:5b (NKJV)

Nana's Hat

Isn't Nana the most wonderful name next to Mommy? I love it! I love that it stands for extra kisses and hugs.

I am so excited! As I write, Julie is in her last week of pregnancy. Come this Saturday, I will be a nana again. I watched her the other day as we were having much-needed pedicures. She just glowed as she talked about the upcoming delivery of her child. Isn't God just grand! He not only has allowed me to be a mother, but a grandmother; that's what we are—grand mothers! I love being a grandmother (I'm Nana to our grandbabies). It seems that you have so much more time, or at least take extra time for those precious little ones. You want to make them feel so good about themselves and so special. They are added extra special blessings from God.

Noah was the first baby who called me Nana. He is the child of my cousin Gerald and his then wife, Dawn. Dawn had no family close by, and her mother had passed away from cancer. My heart went out to her, and we soon called her one of our own. When Noah was born, I went over to their house every night to rock him to sleep. He was my shoulder baby. He would fall asleep on my shoulder every time, and I would lay him down for a good night's rest. He was and is a lot of fun to be around. As he grew, my love for him grew. I feel so blessed to be a part of his life. When he was a toddler, we would go to Pal's (a local drive-thru), get a biscuit, and just sit in the car and talk and eat. I took him out of his car seat and let him sit up front with me. He loved it. Isn't it strange how the little things we share are the most treasured? I put music in the CD player that the junior choir sang, and before long, Noah knew every one of the songs. We did a group of songs called Hallelujah Hop, and when it came time for us to perform at church, he was right up there with the rest of them. He was only two or three at the time. He's almost ten now, plays football, and still loves to sing, even though he might not admit it.

Noah was not to be the only child born to Gerald and Dawn. Annie was born a month after my mother passed away, and on the date of my father's death. I know that God placed her on this earth for me, if for no one else. We share a very special bond of love that can't be broken. From the beginning, she was a happy baby. She loves to snuggle and cuddle and has the sweetest smile. Just the other day, she spent the night with us, and as always, slept in our bed, right in the middle, all snuggled up. She always wakes with a smile, and this one particular morning I asked her if she had slept comfortably. She replied yes and then added, "Nana, do you know what the most comfortable thing in your house is?" I told her no. She said, "It's you and my papaw." What a beautiful thing to be called—comfortable. To me, that meant she felt she belonged here, loved and secure.

And then along came Abbie, the youngest sibling in the Eidson family. She is a character all to herself. She is the bravest child I know. She has beautiful sparkling blue eyes and dark hair and a grin that will melt your heart. She is not afraid to try anything. She has recently learned to ride her bike without the training wheels and often has a fall. She gets up before you know it and announces, "I'm okay, I'm okay," even before you ask.

I love to take the girls to do girl things. We fix our hair and makeup and go shopping and have manicures, and of course eat at Fazoli's, where we have spaghetti and turtle cheesecake. The place we have our manicures done also does pedicures. Abbie told me one day she wanted to get her feet wet like Nana, so the next time we went, she got her feet wet too.

Garrett Luke Smith was born on October 26, 2005 (more about his birth in the next chapter). When Julie brought this beautiful baby into the world, it was one of the happiest days of my life. He was adorable. He was dark skinned with jet black, thick hair. Our pastor said he had never seen a baby with so much hair. He looked as if he could use a haircut when he was first born. He would hold his head up by himself and was so alert even after just a few days. He is truly a joy.

He is almost two now and can go and do just about anything. He talks a mile a minute. He loves to dance and play the pic-ar (guitar) like Uncle

Jimmy. He sings "Achy-Breaky Heart" and "Jesus Loves Me." He can make me laugh until I cry. Julie and Shannon said they don't watch TV anymore. They just watch Garrett. He is the entertainment. He loves to ride with me on my clown scooter. We go through the neighborhood looking for turtles and birds. He notices everything. He loves tractors and motorcycles, Oreo cookies, and M & M's.

Garrett smiles with his eyes. They just twinkle with love and mischief. He is the first grandchild on both sides of the family. Of course, none of us spoil him. I know that I will enjoy watching him grow in the grace and goodness of God.

When I wrote the beginning of the chapter, Julie was expecting our second grandchild. He's here! Another boy! Alan James Smith is a beautiful baby. Of course I would think so, I'm the nana. He is almost three months old now and beginning to ooo and coo. When he smiles, he has a cute little dimple on his right cheek. He loves to be held, and I do that as much as possible. It's my job to love and spoil them—and then send them home.

Garrett and Alan visit us several days a week. I am so blessed! I know I say this a lot, but I am!

There are so many children who don't have a nana and a papaw who love them, and there are so many people who don't have the pleasure of having children or grandchildren. God has blessed me above measure. He has given me the very desires of my heart, beyond what I ever dreamed possible. He is such a loving, giving, caring God.

From those to whom much is given, much is required, and I hope and pray that I will be the nana who serves God. My prayer is that one day I will get to see each grandchild come to know Jesus in his heart. I want these grandchildren to see in their nana's life the Jesus who loves them so. I want them to see love and joy that overflows and spills into their lives. I want to be the nana who is there for them not only in good times but in bad times and let them know that an ever-present God is always there for them.

I'm sure there is a lot more to say about being a nana, but the best thing I can say is that I am proud and honored to be one. I am humbled by my God for allowing me such a privilege, and I thank him each day for his abundant love.

If you're a nana, I know you feel as I do. If you're not a nana, find a child to be a nana to.

Every child can use a comforting lap to climb into, a hug to make him feel secure, and a smile to brighten her day.

If God has given you a special gift to love and minister to children, then by all means, start using that gift! Don't put it off. You are missing the greatest blessing you will ever be given.

//

Behold, children are a heritage from the Lord, The fruit of the womb is a reward.

Psalm 127:3 (NKJV)

But when Jesus saw it, He was greatly displeased and said to them, "Let the little children come to Me, and do not forbid them; for of such is the kingdom of God."

Mark 10:14 (NKJV)

Miracle of Life and Death

I guess this is the hardest chapter to write because it reminds me how fragile life can be. This part of my journey started on a Sunday afternoon in October of 2005. I had been having some trouble with a pulled tendon in my left leg and was wearing an aircast boot. Annie came home with us that afternoon, and we watched *The Lion King* in my bedroom while I painted her fingernails and toenails. I promised Annie I would curl her hair for church that night after I finished getting ready. I started to walk back to the bedroom, and as I passed through the bathroom door, the most excruciating pain I have ever experienced shot up my left leg. It felt as though someone had stuck a broomstick up my foot and into my lower leg. I must have hollered because Annie came running to help me. She managed to help me get back to the bedroom. I knew something awful had happened, yet I did not want to scare her. She was only five. With Annie's help, we got my boot back on. I fixed her hair as I had promised, somehow drove to church, left her with Julie, and told Jim we needed to go to the hospital. X-rays were taken at the hospital, but they could not really tell how much injury there was to my foot and leg. I had an appointment with my podiatrist on Tuesday, so I elected to wait until then to see what needed to be done.

I of course decided to go to work on Monday. My boss told me she knew I was in trouble when I walked in wearing the boot and using the walker my mother had. I saw my podiatrist on Tuesday. He immediately sent me to an orthopedic surgeon, who looked at my X-rays and gave me the bad news. My Achilles tendon had come completely away from the bone, and the only way to fix it was to replace it with a donor tendon. I was to have outpatient surgery on Friday, October 7.

As most of you probably know, hospitals rarely keep patients overnight for anything these days. I was sent home after surgery that afternoon with pain medication and told to keep my foot elevated for forty-eight hours. I was sick on the way home, and the back of my leg and foot felt as though they were sitting in a hot fire of coals. I commented to Jim that if hell were even a tenth that hot, I would not want to go. I was given Percocet for pain. It did not even touch the pain, plus I had a reaction to it that made me itch. The pain was so severe that I was literally pulling my hair and crying out in pain. I begged Jim to take me to the hospital. He finally called my niece Michelle, a registered nurse in the emergency room of our local hospital, and she gave us some advice as to what else I could take for the pain. I finally drifted off to sleep, and the next day Jim called the doctor, and a new medication was ordered. The next few days, I kept the foot elevated and tried to tolerate the pain.

On the following Thursday, October 13, I had breakfast, and Jim helped me clean up and get situated back in bed. My faithful dog, Lillie (a beautiful white Spitz) stayed by my side on the bed, just keeping me company. I will never forget what happened next. Have you ever held a hamster or little mouse in your hand and felt its tiny feet move around? That is similar to the feeling I had. I felt as though something was crawling up through my body, and then it stopped in my chest. I immediately was short of breath and weak and wondered how long it would be before I could not breathe.

Lillie immediately laid her head on my chest and would not move. She sensed something was wrong. I hollered at Jim and told him to be calm but to dial 911. I could tell by the look on his face he was scared, and he asked me again what to do. I told him again to be calm and dial 911. When the ambulance arrived, they checked me out, asked if I was having chest pain, etc. I told them I was short of breath, no chest pain, and that I thought it was a blood clot, not a heart attack.

Michelle was working in the ER that day and knew that something had to be terribly wrong for us to have called an ambulance. I began to have pain in my upper right shoulder, and it became worse the longer I was there. I was taken to the X-ray department to have a CT scan and told to raise my arms. I was in so much pain that I thought I would probably die during the test. The fear was confirmed; I had a bilateral pulmonary embolism, and I was not doing well. By this time, Jimmy had arrived from Maryville, sixty miles away, along with the rest of my family. The decision was made to move me to a larger facility approximately forty-five minutes away. Although no one really said how bad my condition was, I knew it was not good. Michelle rode with me to the hospital, and when Jim asked her later why the sirens were on all the way, she tried to ease his mind and tell him it was just so that we could get there a little faster. She didn't tell him that I might die before we got there.

When we arrived at Holston Valley, I knew it was worse than I even thought. They wheeled me straight to CCU (critical care unit). People came from every direction, poking me, hooking me up to machines. Doctors and nurses were everywhere. I tried to make light of the situation and told them I had brought my own registered nurse with me. They didn't think that was funny.

Everything went steadily downhill from there. Nothing relieved the pain I was having in my right shoulder. It radiated from my shoulder to the middle of my chest. I became nauseated. I had a reaction to morphine. My breathing became worse. I began to swell, and my arms began to bruise from lack of blood flow. My blood pressure continued to drop, and by Thursday night my liver and kidneys were beginning to fail. My family was told I might have a chance to survive if I lived through the night. My condition was extremely critical. The cast on my leg was cut open to relieve pressure from the swelling. I drifted in and out of consciousness all night and the next day. By Friday, my blood pressure dropped even more, and the damage to my lungs worsened. My family was called to my bedside and told that I needed to be put on life support. The outlook was grim. The last thing I can remember before losing complete consciousness was seeing my family crying. Jim just stood and sobbed, Julie called out, "Mom," and Jimmy spoke as if he were a little child—he called me Mama. My mind could not comprehend what was taking place, and I wondered why everyone was so upset. I thought I was moving to another room. I certainly didn't realize I might be moving to a room in heaven.

The next day came, and someone told me I had to wake up. I woke up all right; with two tubes down my throat and my arms tied to the bed. I had no idea what had happened. Jim said I had a look of terror on my face. Since I could not talk, I tried to communicate with a pencil and paper. I thought I must have passed out. Jim tried to explain to me what had happened. I wrote on the piece of paper the words, "This is bad." He broke down in tears and had to leave the room.

Julie tried to make things better and showed me a picture the children had sent with the words, "We love you, Nana." She told me I had to get better for them. Julie also showed me a heart-shaped balloon and asked if I knew who it was from. I immediately knew it was from Eddie Linkous, one of the members of our clown group. I knew the story he told about this heart, and without ever saying a word, he had sent me a wealth of encouragement and love. Little is much when God is in it!

My arms and hands ached and were black and swollen beyond recognition. When I looked down, I thought I was in someone else's body—not mine. I soon learned that my liver and kidneys had shut down. My liver function slowly returned, and in the days to follow I would begin kidney dialysis.

During all this time, friends and family had gathered in the ICU waiting room. Word had spread quickly that I was at the point of death. Hundreds—no, I would say thousands—of prayers went to the Lord on my behalf. My family and I were showered with continual love and support.

I remember very little of the next few days. On Sunday, the tubes were removed and I had a few visitors. The ones I remember were the ones who spoke my name over and over. Somehow, that seemed to get my attention. I could only speak in a low whisper. Our pastor and music director came in to see me. We have a certain phrase our church would say. The pastor would say, "God is good," and we would respond with, "All the time." Then it would be reversed and we would say, "All the time," and he would say, "God is good." That day, my pastor said those words to me, and in the midst of my condition I whispered back, "All the time," and, "God is good."

He is good. He is excellent. He is steadfast and unmovable. He was with me all of those days in the hospital. I never doubted he was there.

On Monday, I was moved down the hall to a room. I was still in critical care but stable. I was so very weak and so very sick. When they brought a tray for me to eat, Jim tried to feed me and encouraged me to eat. I would take a few bites and minutes later throw up. Later he told me that he was afraid if I did not eat, I would not get stronger and maybe not be able to come home. I think his greatest fear was the possibility of putting me in a nursing home.

Dialysis was horrible. For one thing, I was terrified because I didn't know what to expect. My family was not allowed into the room where I was having dialysis because there might be other patients in there as well. They inserted a temporary line into my groin area for the dialysis, and then I was told to lie completely still and especially not to cough. Well, they might as well have told me to jump up and down on the bed! I still had to suction the fluid out of my lungs, and that fluid made me cough horribly. Almost every time I coughed, the machine made a noise and shut down, and the tubing came loose. The nurse would come in and with both hands mash down on my groin area and move the tubing back in place. It was so much fun!

Oh, and did I mention at this point, smells made me deathly ill as well. Each time she reached over me to work on the machine or me, I thought I would puke on top of her. And on top of all that, it was hot in there. Sweat poured off my forehead. This procedure took about four hours each day, but my kidneys began to heal slowly. My urine output was measured each day. I remember that Jim was so excited when after several days there was a trickle of water to be measured. We were told that I had to have measurable output before the kidneys would even start to heal. It was a good sign, but I was not out of the woods.

Each day the kidney specialist came in, and each day I asked if I had to have dialysis again. I dreaded it so. At one point, my niece had learned that my kidneys actually got worse instead of better. I thought this might be a permanent procedure I would have to live with, and the very thought of that made me even more sick. After three days of treatments, I was again told by the doctors that they would have to wait and see.

That night my body and mind were totally exhausted. I did not feel as though I could endure any more. I cried and told Jim that I just could not go through another treatment. As I tried to go to sleep that night, I thought and thought about it. Just who did I think I was? There were a lot of people who had to be on dialysis their entire lives.

Did I think I was better than they were? I prayed and told God that if I had to endure this horrible treatment, that I was willing to do so. I just wanted to have peace about it and let him know my life was his and he could do with it whatever he needed to. It was as though a great weight was lifted, and I felt a tingling from my toes to the top of my head. The next morning when the doctors came in, I was told there would be no more dialysis. Praise the Lord! He is such a great physician! God didn't want me to run a marathon; he just wanted me to be a willing servant.

During all this time, my little Julie was carrying our first grandchild and was due any day. She was faithful to stay by my side, wipe my face, hold my hand, and love me. I was concerned for her. Her feet and hands were swollen, but she did not want to leave me. Jim and the children were able to get a room in the hospital, where they could rest or spend the night. Julie went to the doctor on October 25 and came back with the news that her baby would be delivered on the next day. She would be on the floor above me.

The next morning Julie, Shannon, Jimmy, and Jim sat at my bedside. I had so longed for this moment to be with Julie at her side when her first child and my first grandchild was to be born. I wanted to be able to comfort her as only a mother can do in those times and let her know how wonderful a journey she was about to begin with her new bundle of joy. But it was not to be. I had resigned myself to the fact I would not be with her, but I knew someone who would. Before we had prayer that morning, I held Julie's hand and told her that I knew I could not be there physically next to her, but I told her that God was the bridge that held my hand and her hand on the floor above and that he was always there.

Technology is wonderful these days. Thank God for cell phones! Besides Shannon and Julie, Jim and I were the first ones to hear Garrett Luke Smith's first cry in this world. Shannon was able to call us downstairs. What a blessing for me! Everyone took pictures and video and brought them down to show me this precious little boy. I know God has great plans for him. He has already made his mark in this world and is so precious to us.

The next day was even more wonderful than the birth of my new grandson. It was the day I first held him in my arms. I was so weak yet so very happy that the Lord had allowed me to live one more day and see yet another miracle. All kinds of red tape had to be cut so that Julie and Garrett could come down to see me. It was one of the most wonderful days of my life.

After things calmed down a bit from the excitement of a new baby, the task of recovery began again. I was still so sick and could not keep anything in my stomach. I was given what I call milkshake in a bag. They called it nutrition. I had not eaten any solid food for almost three weeks. Some of the reason I was so sick was that my kidneys were not filtering out toxins and poisons in my system. I really don't know the other reasons. I just know that any smells made me deathly ill and food was the last thing I wanted to see. Finally, I was given a drug called Raglan, and that did the trick. I was able again to eat.

There were so many things that seemed so hard for me. I was extremely weak. As the swelling and fluid went away, my body ached. Sometimes the slightest touch from someone was painful. One day I was taken to surgery to have a new PICC line inserted. I had been stuck so many times that there weren't any good veins left for IVs, and I was still being given antibiotics, fluids, etc. It seemed as though every day was a new challenge.

Jim was the best nurse I had. He rarely left me and knew what I needed even before I did. He took on the task of bathing me every day. I was so weak that most of the time I could not even move to help him. This was, of course, the nurse's job, but after one of them had started the job one day and did not come back to finish bathing me after an hour, Jim became the head nurse. He changed sheets, brushed my hair, helped brush my teeth. Not once did he complain. He cried when I cried, slept in a chair, and loved me into getting better. How blessed I am to have a man who loves me and took his wedding vows to heart: "In sickness and in health." He just wasn't ready for the "until death do us part" part of the vows. He never gave up on me, and I know that it is because of his love and care for me, and God's mercy, that I am still here.

There were many struggles yet to endure in my recovery. To begin with, I remember thinking one day as Jim's sister sat in a chair in front of me, *I will never be strong enough to even stand, much less sit in a chair like a normal person again.* How much I longed to be a "normal" person. I certainly won't forget the first time I was told I had to stand and take a few steps. It was horrible. The physical therapist said she had been told I was afraid to walk. Are you kidding? Who wouldn't be? I had been bedridden, nearly lost my life, and now told I was afraid. The fact was that I was so weak that my body didn't want to walk. I was in agony. I kept telling her I was going to pass out, but she wouldn't listen. When they finally sat me down in a chair, my blood pressure had dropped to eighty over forty! Needless to say, she didn't come back. Before that was tried again, I was given a chance to gain some strength.

When I was finally able to eat again, I was moved to another room. A room with a view! The room that I had been in for so long had a window but only a view of the brick wall of the building next door. IVs were eventually removed, and I was able to sit in a chair for an hour at a time. Things were looking up.

Now back to the original problem I had: my foot. When it began to swell, the doctors had cut my cast and then wrapped it back with an Ace bandage. Afterward, each time my foot was moved, the heel rubbed against the cast. This caused a decubitus ulcer, which was completely black and about the size of the bottom of a coffee cup. No one, of course, wanted to take the blame for this problem.

Although it seems like one problem or another would arise, I was getting better, and the day finally came when I was released from the hospital. I was determined to at least walk on my own to the door of my room before getting back into a wheelchair. With God's help, I did. It was a beautiful day. The sun was shining. The air had a sweet aroma, even through the stench of pollution. I believe God cleared the air long enough for me to smell life again. I couldn't believe I was finally going home! All my family were there to greet me with "Welcome home" signs. It was a glorious day. Tears of joy streamed down my face. I held my new grandbaby in my arms for what seemed forever. New life and a life spared! God is so good!

I will not tell you that my recovery has been easy. It has by no means been easy. I have been discouraged, depressed, and downhearted many, many times. And there are still times today that I get discouraged. My life has changed. I am no longer physically able to work. I did return for about a year, but it was just too much. I walk with a cane because of the damage and weakness in my leg. And after almost three years, the ulcer on my foot is still healing. Physically I will never be the same, but spiritually I have grown more than I ever thought possible. I have a new love for the Lord, a new appreciation for life. We are not promised tomorrow. It is a gift from God.

A day or so after I was so critical, Jim asked me this question: "Did you see a bright light when you were so close to dying?" My answer was no. My family was told I was going to die; but my God had other plans for me. When I was unaware of those around me and so close to death's door, there was incredible peace. Wherever I was, was the most peaceful place I have ever been. There was no pain, no sadness. I did not go to heaven or to heaven's gate, but I believe with all my heart that Jesus was holding me in the palm of his hand, sheltering me from pain. It was like a father holds his child in his arms, the safest place I could have been. For reasons that only God knows, my work on earth was not finished, and he has allowed me to stay a little longer.

Even though I have been a Christian for

many years, I think I feared death because it was unknown. I no longer have that fear, but rather a longing more for heaven than I had before. I'm not in a hurry to die, yet I can't wait to see Jesus and feel those arms around me once more, welcoming me home.

The best way I can describe my experience has already been told in the Bible in Psalm 23.

> Yea, though I walk through the valley of the shadow of death, I will fear no evil; For You are with me; Your rod and Your staff, they comfort me. You prepare a table before me in the presence of my enemies; You anoint my head with oil; My cup runs over. Surely goodness and mercy shall follow me. All the days of my life; And I will dwell in the house of the Lord forever.

I was only in the *valley of the shadow* of death, being held in Jesus's arms. I thank God for my valley.

Future Hats and a Crown

Death is no respecter of persons. I don't know how many times I have heard this from preachers in funerals and in church services. It's true. Age doesn't matter. Young and old both die. Sometimes it is from an illness that has ravished a body for a long time, and death is somewhat a relief to the family because their loved one has suffered for so long. Other times, it is sudden, without warning. Sometimes it is from an accident, a child hit by a car, or someone drowns. Death comes in many shapes and forms. It may be unexpected by us, but it is never unexpected by God. He is never caught off guard by death. I believe he is saddened by our grief and is there to wrap his loving arms around us if we will just let him.

In John 11:1–44, we are told how Jesus himself wept at the sight of the death of his dear friend Lazarus. He loved this family, and when he became sick, they sent word for Jesus to come. He did not come right away and made the statement that his sickness was not unto death, but for the glory of God, that the Son of God might be glorified through it. Family members questioned his death, the same way we often do when death or sickness comes to our loved ones. Lazarus had been dead for four days. Mary cried out and told Jesus if he had just been there, Lazarus would not have died. He grieved with these family members. The Bible tells us that his grief and sadness was so that he groaned in himself.

His love for this dear family compelled him to raise Lazarus from the dead. He knew that God would be glorified in the performing of this miracle. He asked that the stone be taken away. And then Jesus lifted up his eyes and said, "Father, I thank you that you have heard me. And I know that you always hear me, but because of the people who are standing by I said this, that they may believe that you sent me." He cried with a loud voice, "Lazarus, come forth!" And Lazarus came forth in his graveclothes, totally bound head and foot. Even his face was wrapped with a cloth. Jesus said to those around him, "Loose him, and let him go." Can you imagine the testimony Lazarus had? "I was dead, but now I'm alive! *Alive!*"

So many times, we as Christians are bound by this world; whether it be sickness, sorrow, pride, or any number of things. We need to be loosed and let go of whatever holds us from being all that we can be for Jesus and his kingdom.

Not long after Jesus performed the miracle of raising Lazarus from his grave, he himself would be ridiculed, arrested, and put on trial for being just who he was—the son of God. He certainly deserved none of the shame, humiliation, pain, and suffering that he endured. Yet he gave his life willingly so that all of us might be forgiven for all the sins in our lives. No one took his life. *It was given freely.* Why? Because he loved us just as he loved Lazarus. His love for us is no different. He weeps with us when we weep, he hurts when we hurt, and he rejoices when we rejoice. He wants his children to be near him and to have a daily relationship with him. Each day we wake up, we talk with those around us. We tell each other good morning, ask how they are doing, listen to problems, and laugh with each other. Don't we know that Jesus wants us to have that same closeness with him? All we have to do is talk to him. I know myself that sometimes I make that so hard. I feel that he is so big and so far away; but he isn't. He is always here, wherever I am. Even as I write these words, Jesus guides me.

I don't know what my future holds or how long my future on earth may be. But I do know, without any doubt, who holds that future. I may wear many more hats. Jesus has blessed me with such wonderful hats so far that I know whatever hats he has in store for me will bring me closer to him. For sure, I will have many more miracles because each day brings the miracle of life. Each of us has been given the gift of life, yet we are not promised another day. What we do with our lives is up to us. Will we accept Jesus as our personal Savior, or will we deny him and live a life that is bound up in this world?

The last hat that I plan on wearing is a crown. Let's just consider a minute the meaning of the word *crown* and how it all began. A crown is described as a special headdress worn by royalty and other persons of high merit and honor. In the Old Testament, David's crown was a prize of battle (2 Samuel 12:30). As a symbol of his authority, the crown was worn when the king was on his throne and when leading his forces in combat (2 Samuel 1:10). The word *crown* was also used figuratively, referring to the old man's gray head (Proverbs 16:31), a man's virtuous wife (Proverbs 12:4), and God's blessings on mankind (Psalm 8:5). Occasionally the word referred to a festive wreath of leaves or flowers (Song of Solomon 3:11).

In the New Testament it usually has a figurative significance. Paul envisioned "a crown of righteousness" for himself and others (2 Timothy 4:8), and James anticipated "the crown of life" (James 1:12). While the winning runner of that day received a garland of myrtle leaves, Paul looked forward to a crown that would not decay (1 Corinthians 9:25). Not even the victorious athlete would receive his reward unless he obeyed the rules (2 Timothy 2:5). Conversely, the word evokes revulsion when we read of Roman soldiers weaving briers into a crown for Jesus's head (Matthew 27:29).

In the book of Revelation, crowns are both realistic and figurative. The twenty-four elders seated around God's throne were wearing "crowns of gold" (Revelation 4:4), and as they worshiped, they "cast their crowns before the throne" (Revelation 4:10) (Reference: The Holman Bible Dictionary for crown).

The crown that the apostles speak of is the incorruptible crown, the crown of life (James 1:12; Revelation 2:10) "that fadeth not away" (1 Peter 5:4) (Easton's Bible Dictionary).

I look forward to wearing that crown of life and righteousness that Paul and James spoke of: a crown that is incorruptible and will never fade away; a crown I can lay at my Jesus's feet and thank him for shedding his blood on an old rugged cross just for me.

Do you know this Jesus today? As you can tell from my story, he is the best friend I have and ever will have. We all wear different hats, and we never know from day to day what hat we will be wearing. With God as our hatmaker, we can be assured our hats will always fit correctly. My prayer for each of you is to invite Jesus into your heart today, so one day you too can wear the greatest hat of all—the crown of life, everlasting and eternal!

clementineclown@charter.net

listen|imagine|view|experience

AUDIO BOOK DOWNLOAD INCLUDED WITH THIS BOOK!

In your hands you hold a complete digital entertainment package. In addition to the paper version, you receive a free download of the audio version of this book. Simply use the code listed below when visiting our website. Once downloaded to your computer, you can listen to the book through your computer's speakers, burn it to an audio CD or save the file to your portable music device (such as Apple's popular iPod) and listen on the go!

How to get your free audio book digital download:

1. Visit www.tatepublishing.com and click on the e|LIVE logo on the home page.
2. Enter the following coupon code:
   b93f-2043-de1b-d8b6-57ed-250b-526b-834d
3. Download the audio book from your e|LIVE digital locker and begin enjoying your new digital entertainment package today!